Rail Mail

A Century of American Railroading on Picture Postcards

By Geoff Stunkard

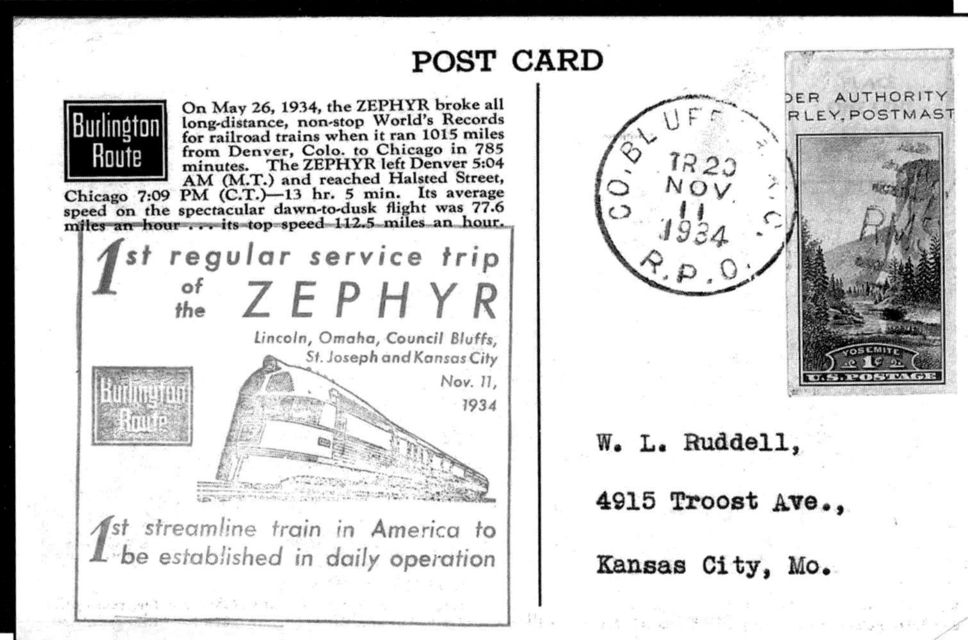

Stunkard, Geoffrey F., 1963-
Rail Mail: A century of American railroading on picture postcards, including information on buying, selling, and collecting postcards.

Includes bibliography

ISBN: 0-9748216-0-8

1. Railroads - American - History - Pictorial Works 2. Postcards - Railroads - History   3. Antiques - Postcards - Railroad
385.097

Graphic Design: Geoff Stunkard
Printing: Sabre Printers/Overmountain Press - Johnson City, TN

To Dad and Linda -
  thanks for making all of this possible...

INQUIRIES/RETAIL & CLUB ORDERS -
Quarter Milestones Publishing
P.O. Box 441
Milligan College, TN 37682-0441
(423) 542-0159
    email- qmp@preferred.com
BOOKSTORE & WHOLESALE (800) 992-2691

FRONTPIECE - The fabled *Burlington Zephyr*, the train credited with birthing the diesel passenger age, on a postcard issued for its first run in regular service. Above left is the 1934 RPO cancel on the back of the same card showing this particular train.

ON THE COVER - Among the most famous of the daylight limiteds that plied the rails was the Jersey Central's *Blue Comet*, which ran between the suburbs of northern New Jersey and the Atlantic shore. It is seen here on a scarce postcard issued during the early 1930s.

3/04 FIRST EDITION - FIRST PRINTING of 2500

Ben Hur Terminal Station, Crawfordsville, Ind.

Like all such addictions, this one began simply enough. While pursuing paper memorabilia for auto racing research, I began to attend postcard shows on a friend's recommendation. The almost complete lack of racing material found me searching for other subjects as an aside, the primary one being trains. This was the result of a lifelong interest in railroading initiated by my father, who worked as a corporate traffic manager for 30 years.

As I began pursuing railroad postcards, the more I saw, the more intrigued I became. Each opportunity to view new postcard stock still seems to reveal previously-unknown treasures. Finding a card signed by a railroad president or of a rare construction scene is a thrill that never goes away. The racing interest remains, but the railroad postcards now get the most attention from a collecting standpoint.

Deltiology, or the hobby of collecting postcards, is a fascinating one. There exists an immense variety of railroad-related cards produced during the last 100 years or so; an honest estimate would probably be somewhere in the neighborhood of a quarter-to-half million different views. Some people collect a variety of rail-related subjects, while others may specialize in a single railroad or region.

Picture postcards, which first became part of the postal landscape in the 1890s, have served many purposes throughout their existence. For the railroads, these included notification and documentation, but their primary purpose was promotional. America's railroad systems used postcards extensively during the first half of the last century. It allowed them to put both illustration and name recognition together on a subliminal advertising item that was personalized by the sender and certain to be read by the recipient.

While postcards could be used to promote new equipment and services to potential shippers, the railroad postcard was used much more often to promote the luxury passenger services a rail line offered to the riding public. Views of engines, new train consists and well-appointed interiors were all used to help bring in new customers. Hundreds of different views of scenery along the railroad routes were published as well.

At present, the larger railroads here in North America have consolidated down into a handful of 'super systems' whose primary goal is the movement of freight; vintage postcards can offer a glimpse into the heritage of passenger travel of bygone times. They give enthusiasts and collectors the opportunity to look into a never-to-be-repeated time in American culture. A trip by rail was (and, to a lesser extent, remains today) a vacation in itself, a chance to relax and be away from the situations encountered in everyday life.

Despite the literal inroads of the automotive industry during the period preceding World War II, rail transportation was still a primary means of travel for most Americans. Railroads nationwide had redundant or duplicating service to many larger parts of the nation. It was therefore up to their public relations and marketing departments to decide how best to get the customers to ride on *their* trains as opposed to a competitor's. In most cases, railroad dining cars actually operated at a loss, with culinary fare designed to ensure that the rail-captive patron left their train feeling that he or she had enjoyed a special dining experience. New equipment was often given as much publicity as possible as well, even being demonstrated on another company's rail corridor on occasion.

In terms of distribution, sometimes these postcards were sold in sets, while others were presented gratis to those actually riding the trains. Many other postcards were done privately, and these normally came from local sources like dime stores and stationery shops. Small firms and regional photographers set out to document stations and trackside views, and occasionally had the good (?) fortune of issuing a card of a local railroad accident. By the end of the century's opening quarter, virtually any postcard documenting major industry had some form of rail transportation visible as well. Seen as the lifelines of American commerce, in this light the rails represented what was good about the 'other side of the tracks.'

Unlike the current era of video games and Internet access, the common ground for many in smaller towns was the railroad station, and sometimes crowds gathered there when the daily train was due to arrive, regardless of whether anyone they knew was on board. In a way, the railroad line actually offered an even greater sense of community, joining all of these smaller locales together. Because of their historic significance to these places, station postcards are often in demand by a much wider audience than rail enthusiasts.

Those readers who are already railroad buffs are likely aware of the impact the railroads had in so much of the nation's growth. They were huge, grandiose enterprises that employed thousands of people and invested billions of dollars in equipment and business. Communities along their routes benefited from local enterprises in agriculture, manufacturing, natural resources, and other commodities that relied on rail transport. Postcards documented all of that as well.

Due to the vast number of cards produced, any attempt to document railroading on postcards would need to be an overview of these cards rather than an exhaustive accounting. Therefore, the purpose of this book is threefold. First of all, it will give the reader an introduction to these cards: their origination, use, and variety. Second, it will serve as an illustrated reference to the various eras and styles of railroad postcards. Finally, it will offer information on postcard collecting in general to aid individuals actively desiring to collect, buy, and sell railroad postcards. A section listing additional resources and books on railroad and postcard history is included, as well as the author's estimated current values on the cards used to illustrate this book.

As one might imagine, choosing which cards to use in a project like this is difficult; there are dozens of other postcards that would certainly have been worthy of inclusion had space been available. Then again, showing every wonderful card ever made might spoil some of the excitement if the reader decides he or she would like to pursue this hobby at greater length; treasures still abound at shows and in antique venues. Since beauty is in the eye of the beholder, I have selected what I felt represented the national scene most vividly, as well as presenting other cards that personally fuel my own collecting passion. Hopefully, you too will appreciate the overall balance.

Although not as predominant in everyday life as they once were, railroads continue to hold a great deal of attraction to the general public. *The Metropolitan Corridor*, as Harvard professor John Stilgoe so aptly described the railroad infrastructure in his book by the same title, was a streak of modernism that ran through a rural nation at the turn of the last century. Its veins and sinews helped America grow into what it became: the leader of the free world. Though the rails are now gone in many places, the magic remains. Collecting postcards is one way to appreciate that.

Geoff Stunkard
March 2004

Special Acknowledgments

I still haven't concluded whether I was momentarily brilliant or simply naïve when I decided to self-publish this book. To complete this project, special thanks goes out to Miriam Stunkard and Rebecca Riley, who looked over the text and helped with the editing; to Edna Lowry, whose assistance in getting the project off the ground financially made this volume possible; to the Rev. Bob Lowry, my father-in-law, who gave sound advice and opened doors of opportunity; to Beth Wright and the crew at The Overmountain Press for encouragement and direction; and to my wonderful wife, Linda, who put up with the hours and one-track mind *Rail Mail* required. And, finally, to George Stunkard, my father, who got this whole railroad thing started in the first place…

America's railroad age was in its heyday at the turn of the Twentieth Century. For millennia, people had needed either animal power or active waterways to move rapidly from one locale to another; now, steel rail was connecting it all together. The world was becoming a smaller place as a result, but the opportunities were now unlimited if one desired to get out and travel. Some who could not afford a ticket took the

These three cards are examples of images from the pre-1907 era featuring crack passenger trains. At top is a limited (possibly on the M-K-T line) leaving St. Louis Union Station, complete with a message from the sender on the front. Below that is an early card showing the record-breaking New York - Chicago Flyer on the Pennsylvania Railroad, predecessor of the famed Broadway Limited. At bottom is a card advertising a visit from a representative of the Cumpson-Prentiss Coffee Company, showing a flagship train of the New York Central, either the 20th Century Limited or the Empire State Express.

Passenger Train Leaving Union Station, St. Louis, Mo.,

No. 102   The P. R. R. New York-Chicago Flyer.   (The 18-hour train)

daring challenge of hopping aboard a slow freight from the small town to the big city. Railroads employed vast numbers of people directly, and indirectly kept an even greater number of individuals busy in other vocations, from the steelworker to the financier. That railroads would be part of the postcard landscape was a given from the very start.

Pioneer Cards

While the true rage in postcard collecting did not begin until after the turn of the century, there were many uses for postal items of this sort during the latter half of the 19th century. Cards done prior to 1898 are called 'pioneer cards' by collectors and came in a variety of formats. Some mailings were trade cards, advertising a product line. Others were notices of delivery from the railroads, telling a customer that a package or parcel had arrived at the local freight house and was

ready for shipment. A few were actually close to what we now consider to be 'standard' postcards. The true 'pioneer' illustrated postcard era ran from the Chicago's Columbian Exposition of 1893 until 1898. These were cards printed by the U.S. government using a .02 cent postal rate and were not officially named 'postcard,' but 'Souvenir Card' or 'Mail Card.' These were illustrated with lithography.

Then, in May 1898, Congress enacted a law that allowed private firms to print postal cards. The cards have the words 'Private Mailing Card' imprinted on them; they are abbreviated as 'PMC' cards by today's collector. In addition to new images, some earlier cards were reprinted in this fashion. The advent of Rural Free Delivery postal service just after the turn of the century had a major impact on people using postcards for correspondence on a regular basis.

Like many collectibles, the values on historic railroad paper goods are driven by graphic quality. For that reason, there has not been a great deal of interest in the pre-1900 pioneer issues among railroad collectors beyond that of novelty. The giant engines and streamliners of the next century remain in greater demand. As imagined, however, the pre-1900 artifacts are hard to come by, and will be of interest to the more specialized collector. Early trade cards, which were sometimes mailed like postcards, were usually of moderate quality in regards to their design and execution. Like all advertising, the purpose was to

From the beginning, railroads took advantage of the postcard as a tool for shipping information. This was a quick and inexpensive way to notify customers of arrivals, shipments, or in the case of this Illinois & Iowa Car Service Association, servicing fees. Cards of this sort hold little value unless they name a specific railroad a buyer is interested in, or feature a scarce cancellation.

entice the potential customer. Experts consider 1876 (the year of the Philadelphia Centennial) to 1904 to be the era of the trade card, and they faded away as postcards grew in popularity.

While trade cards were sometimes colorful, the shipping notices sent out by railroads were all business. Basically, the name of the rail company and various categories to be filled in by the agent were imprinted on one side, sometimes with the company's logo. The other side was addressed to the recipient. Although graphically lacking, these items are sought out by collectors who are interested in a specific railroad. Some defunct Colorado narrow gauge lines, which boomed in that state's silver era until the financial Panic of 1893, are a good example of this. Also, some of the cards issued by the predecessors of a larger line (such as the Pennsylvania or Burlington) might find a following as well. It should be noted, however, that the lack of graphic design seen on most examples keeps values to a minimum.

The picture postcard boom one hundred years ago has been attributed to a number of factors, such as the advanced color printing processes that came into play as the 19th Century ended. Unlike trade cards, postcards were created to serve a greater purpose in this era before telephones and radios, a practicality which added to their importance. By 1900, post-cards were already starting to proliferate world-wide. However, another change to the United States postal code would have a major bearing on postcard use in this country.

A rare pair of printed lithos showing a trolley accident in Charlton, Massachusetts complete with a 1905 accident date. The interior view of the upended car offers a unique persepective. Recreating an incident like this via offset press was a risk not many small-town suppliers were willing to take, hoping that the cards could be sold when they were first offered for sale literally months after the fact; most such cards are in the real-photo category. These thin cardstock examples were probably done quickly by a local printing company rather than by an overseas firm.

March 1, 1907

The types of postcards available prior to early 1907 had one thing in common - the address took up one side of the card and any correspondence had to be written on the side with the illustration. Collectors call these 'undivided back' (UDB) cards. After Congress enacted changes, a vertical line was added to the un-illustrated back side of the card (effective March 1, 1907) so that both address and message could appear there. By now, the processes used to print the cards ranged from crude black and white lithography, often created locally, to high quality color versions that were often produced over-seas, particularly in Germany. In the case of the color cards, some were actually colored or tinted by hand, a labor-intensive procedure when one considers the millions of cards being created. It was during the 1901-1907 era that the size was standardized to 3.5 x 5.5 inches.

In terms of actual design, the pre-1907 undivided back cards usually had a small amount of white space on the front where a few words could be jotted down. In some cases, used cards turn up today with extensive writing that goes through the card's image, which can understandably diminish the value.

Real Photo Postcards Arrive

Real photo postcards made their introduction during this time period as well. The advent of George Eastman's Kodak camera system had made personal photography much more commonplace. However, railroad action images are rare from this era, since the film capability required perfect sunlight, an extremely steady hand or tripod, and, frankly, a lot of luck. On the other hand, rail depots were found on real photo postcards from almost every town. A chapter in this book

Railroad branchlines had spread quickly across the countryside by the postcard era. Some were marginally profitable, and postcards of these lines may have been the only illustrated items created before the rails came back up after a brief (often unprofitable) existence. Many branchlines are gone today.

As mentioned, in the first years of the century, the railroads began to do immense works. Those most notable were in the vicinity around New York City, where railroads abandoned street trackage and began to go underground to sweeping new terminals. At the cost of millions of dollars, these included deep tunneling beneath rivers, electrification programs for smoke abatement, and huge edifices for passenger service. Again, postcards showing these construction zones, which took literally years to complete, as well as cards of both the old and new terminal buildings, can be found.

Though the railroads themselves would create some cards during this time period, more often then not train postcards were done by local vendors. As a result, many local scenes exist that have little or no significance to the average enthusiast. To the specialized collector, however, they can hold immense interest. Again, the railroad collector might find he or she is competing with individuals collecting local scenes of a hometown or favorite location.

Therefore, it is wise to network with non-railroad postcard collectors and be knowledgable about more then just the specific interest of railroads. With quality cards becoming harder to obtain, good trading material can be worth more than one might imagine. *

focuses on these cards, as depot scenes play a prominent role in the early postcard era. Also found on occasion are real photo images of other structures such as switch towers, portraits of locomotives with the crew posed around the machinery, studio shots of faux rear passenger car platforms, and candid photos of everyday life.

Another facet of railroading during this time period was expansion and upgrading, which was often a real-photo subject. With the internal combustion engine in its infancy and paved roads limited to cobblestones or brick in cities, railroads were the primary means of connecting most towns with others, as well as to industry, ensuring access to raw materials and the shipment of finished products. Soon after a depot went up, so did other structures, such as the mandatory produce elevators in agricultural locales.

6907 CABLE INCLINE UP LOOKOUT MOUNTAIN, TENN.

O ne of the earliest producers of picture postcards was named the Detroit Publishing Company. This firm was noted for both the sheer number of cards it created and the high quality lithography process that was used. William Henry Jackson, perhaps the most famous photographer of the old West, was an early partner in this enterprise, bringing with him some 10,000 negatives from a quarter-century of travel. Many of these images became subjects on postcards and larger pieces of lithographic art that the company created.

The origins of the Detroit Publishing Company's predecessor, the Detroit Photographic Company, are somewhat murky, as there were earlier concerns by that name. The business in question had come to the forefront in 1896 under the tutelage of investor William Livingstone and photographer Edwin Husher. Husher had been astounded by the color reproduction he had seen using a proprietary Swiss process called Photochrom. Unlike previous efforts, which required hand-retouching, this new process yielded continuous tonal color of a black-and-white image via the use of multiple lithographic stones; there were no half-tone dot patterns as seen on color images made today.

These premium litho stones were imported from Bavaria, Germany, coated with a special photo-sensitive chemical and then put

in contact with a photo negative. After exposure to several hours of light, the areas where light passed through the negative would become hardened and the remainder could be washed away by a turpentine-like solution. After a clean-up and final image setting using acid, the stones would be set into perfect register and covered with transparent color inks to be transferred to the paper. Amazingly, it has been estimated that as many 14 such stones using a variety of color hues might have been used to create a single image. When completed, the carefully-done, stone-laid impression was indeed magnificent.

In 1897, Livingstone went to Zurich and bought the exclusive North American licensing rights for the process from the creator, Art Institute Orell Fussli. The Swiss parent company in turn sent a gentleman named Albert Schuler to Detroit to oversee the secretive innovations they had developed. With Jackson on board in 1898, the company produced breathtaking color arrays of many subjects from the private mailing card (PMC) era onward. Railroads, some of which had kept Jackson financially viable through much of the 1890s with commission work, are the subject of many Detroit images. The special printing process was named 'Phostint.'

The exact process that the Detroit Publishing Company used for its postcards and prints has unfortunately been lost; the development of less expensive offset color would lead to the firm's eventual bankruptcy in the middle of the 1920s. Indeed, many postcard views from the 1907-1915 era were cheap knock-offs of images that had first come from DPC. Luckily, through the efforts of Jackson, who was in his 80s at the time of the company's failure, most of the negatives have been preserved for posterity.

Values on Detroit Publishing Company postcards are based on a number of factors, not the least of which is condition. Image quality is normally not an issue on these cards, though some pictures were indeed retouched in later releases. Like all postcards, some sold better than others, but all Phostint cards, regardless of subject, have a certain level of intrinsic beauty that make them special to most postcard collectors.   *

The depot, or railroad station, postcard is perhaps the highest-demand subject in the railroad postcard hobby. Though thousands of different views exist, there is a seemingly automatic market for these cards, and with good reason. In America's less frantic times, the railroad depot played a critical role in many communities. As a nation of primarily rural, isolated outposts before the latter half of the 1800s, the importance of the new form of rail transportation cannot be underestimated. Following the Civil War, the expanding railroads were *the* primary means for moving the population west and expanding the nation. Previously, travel had been limited to canal routes and seasonally-open wagon roads. As the railroads became more prevalent on the American scene, that traffic quickly migrated to this convenient form of transportation.

For towns along the proposed routes, it soon became obvious that you were either on the rail line or would be left behind. Nonetheless, even the most optimistic predictions could not foresee how important these connections would be in the expanding industrial society. A new rail connection and depot was an automatic addition to each populated locale that the rails reached, serving both the community with better access and the rail company with business.

By the time postcards came onto the scene at the turn of the century, a good many of these first structures, particularly in the east, had been rebuilt or otherwise superceded. In those cases, the only post-card images existent will show the later buildings. People looking for older images will have no choice but to hope that a local or journeying photographer exposed a glass plate negative that later was transferred to postcard stock. This happened on occasion. Nonetheless, the Victorian era had brought about some wonderful developments in structural design. Some of these features, such as turrets and roof trim, were part of many depot structures by the time of the first postcard craze.

On the other hand, many larger railroads had also developed standardized structural forms for their lineside buildings. Therefore, a station going up or being rebuilt in one locale may have some fairly generic traits with others along that particular rail line. This was

Here are two examples of union depots. At top is the Pennsylvania's structure at Huntingdon, Pa., which also served the Huntingdon & Broad Top short line. Above is the Grand Rapids Mich, train shed with a Michigan Central train leaving under a plume of smoke. Both were medium-sized depots serving multiple lines.

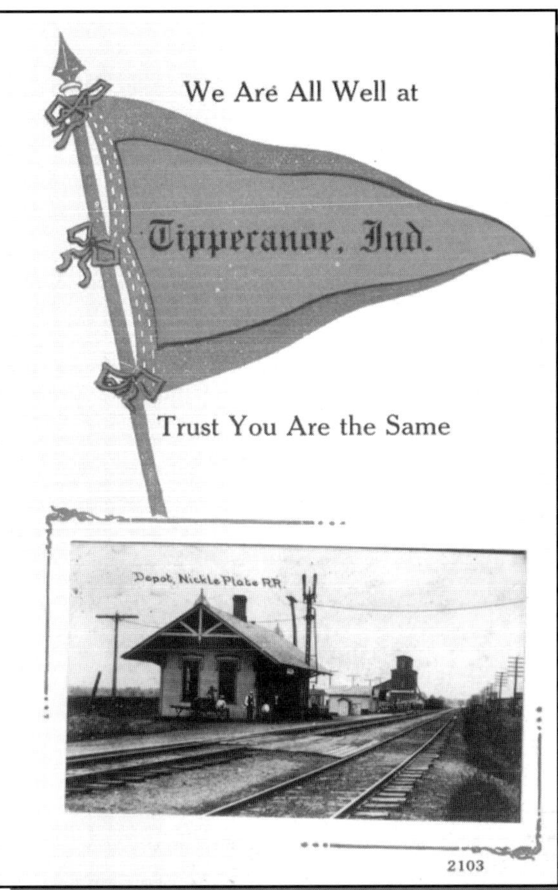

(above) Typical of small-town depots was the structure on the Nickel Plate Railroad at Tippecanoe, Ind. It was destroyed in a 1951 freight train accident.

(right) The Lake Erie & Western (which later became part of the Nickel Plate) structure in Tipton, Ind., made use of stonework and native limestone for its depot. Since Tipton was also a division point with engine facilities before 1933, that may have accounted for this building's sturdiness.

especially true of those roads expanding across the Great Plains and the Southwest. Paint and trim would be somewhat identical along the routes. In these cases, some of the structures bear quite a bit of resemblance to one another. The more ornate or unique railroad depots will often hold more interest to a broader audience of postcard collectors.

The City Terminal

Despite the amount of regulation and taxation the railroads were subjected to, they still had the financial where-with-all to build some of the most impressive structures in the history of American commerce. Except for the huge, dueling Pennsylvania and New York Central edifices in New York City (see p. 20-21), the Union Station concept prevailed in most locales. To build on such a grand scale, the railroads would normally join together to create cavernous edifices in big cities, with many stub-end sidings and monstrous train sheds. The biggest benefactor was the community as a whole, which now needed to go to just one central location to take transportation in any direction. Today, surviving examples of these structures such as Washington

D.C. Union Station, Indianapolis Union Station, and Kansas City Union Station have all been restored, though they are now being used for purposes other than railroading.

Chicago is credited with being the city built by railroads and had six big terminals serving the multiple railroads that went in and out of the Windy City. These included Dearborn, Central, Grand Central, LaSalle Street, Union, and Northwestern. Today, only the Dearborn structure and part of Union Station survive from the days of vintage postcards. Traffic in the region was constant, feeding the nation's resources through the city and its sprawling freight and passenger yards. Several high-speed interurban lines, such as the now-defunct Chicago, North Shore and Milwaukee, also served Chicago, as did Illinois Central's electrified commuter services. The fabled Loop rapid transit system and the Parmelee Transfer company moved transcontinental travelers between the various depots.

The biggest station out on the west coast was the Los Angeles Union Terminal, which has also now been restored. There were sever-al other locations on the western seaboard that also served multiple railroads, but generally railroads were much more spread out west of the Mississippi River, or had greater regional control (like the Southern Pacific north of Los Angeles).

Of all the big city terminals, perhaps the one that has garnered the most acclaim from an existing structural standpoint is the former Cincinnati Union Terminal, which is now that city's art museum and cultural center. Built at the height of the Depression in 1933, it's domed design has been widely heralded as a crowning achievement of the Art Deco movement and remains a piece of classic American architecture to this day.

From a collector's standpoint, the big city terminals hold a marginal interest. In many cases (though not all), examples are very common and can be easily acquired. A collector looking for variations on a particular structure will generally be the only one who has a direct interest in the cards. As with all railroading images, those showing trains are more popular than street-side views, and examples with better graphic design create more interest among collectors.

Small Town Depots

Before the advent of good roads and the personal automobile, the railroad station in most towns was the lifeblood of commerce to that location. The railroad could move virtually any product in or out, took care of the non-local mail and postal movement, and serviced the community's long-distance travel needs. As mentioned, without such opportunities available, a town was isolated. As the railroad routes were laid out, they would often take an unexpected jaunt from a straighter course to reach potential customers, an important considera-

Small town depots like this example at Concordville, PA on the Pennsylvania's Octoraro Branch were commonplace across the nation during the first postcard craze. The structure itself is built of wood, while in the background is the freight depot and the ever-present water tower to keep the boilers of the locomotives well-fed. According to dealer Bill Martin, cards of this nature are among the highest-demand view cards in the postcard collecting hobby.

tion when issuing and selling bonds prior to construction.

The small-town depot is something of a misnomer, as it really encompasses any railroad passenger structure other than a big city terminal or station. The depot could be as small as a lean-to with a train order board (which looked like a semaphore signal) used to stop a local train only when a passenger or freight shipment needed to be picked up. In most towns, however, the station would be a structure with a number of possible rooms, including a clerk's living quarters or offices. In the South there were racially-segregated areas, and nationwide there might be a waiting room reserved for women, where they wouldn't be subjected to the worldly ways of the traveling man. A separate room in the station would hold small freight, and the station master would have an area in the building reserved for the business of railroading, sometimes with a bay window looking out over the rails.

In places where the railroad had a good deal of commerce, a separate freight station might be erected adjacent to or across from the passenger structure. If a road grade crossing was nearby (which was almost always unless the railroad had already built a viaduct or overpass to avoid traffic problems), there may be safety crossing gates or a watchman's shanty. Other peripheral items could include tool sheds and other smaller buildings.

In some instances, the local depot would serve two railroads, and some depots served two or more railroads at a crossing-type junction. This would be where two lines intersected with each other. Places like Durand, Mich., Marion, Ohio, and Joliet, Ill., all fall into this category. There, in addition to the other structures, a switch tower controlling signals and train movement might be built into the station or down the track from this critical area.

The more important a location became, the larger the station. The railroads would upgrade these buildings if traffic or competition warranted such action. As time went on, the union station concept became more prevalent, and passenger rail lines would be be built or rerouted to better serve the community from one central location. Indeed, sometimes a separate terminal or belt railroad was created for and owned by the participating lines at the biggest stations. These switching and transfer trains would serve the passenger station and provide interchange services of cars between the different companies. The Jacksonville (Fla.) Union Terminal line was one such operation.

While most postcard sellers will usually have a number of city terminals in their railroad stock, the small town depot image has a much broader audience. In addition to railroad enthusiasts, the primary buyer will be the locale-specific collector, who is looking for images from a specific town, county or state. As a result, sometimes depot images could be intermixed with that state's cards in a dealer's stock. Prices can vary widely, dependent on the dealer, how popular

LOBBY, UNION TERMINAL, CINCINNATI, OHIO

that particular spot is, the quality of the view, and of course the quality of the card itself. Depot real photo postcards would be at the top of this list, followed by those showing train engines, those showing train tracks and finally those shown from the street.

For the collector, it may be wise to try to locate regional depot cards as far from the actual locale as possible. In other words, Phoenix could be a better place price-wise to buy cards from North Carolina than Charlotte might be. Note, however, that sellers who know this category also know these images will often sell based on their quality, regardless of location. Experienced paper and postcard dealers recognize which locations, regions, and railroad companies sell the best for them, and understandably price their cards accordingly.   *

N.Y.N.H.& H. STATION, BRIDGEPORT, CONN.   91722

The New Grand Central Depot, 42nd Street, New York.

INTERIOR, PENNSYLVANIA STATION, NEW YORK CITY — 73 — K 4867

PENNSYLVANIA STATION, NEW YORK CITY

Of all the big-city terminals that came into being worldwide, few can equal the structures built by the competing New York Central and Pennsylvania Railroad lines in New York City. By the turn of the century, the Big Apple was sprawling. The scoffers who had laughed when the Central's 'Commodore' Cornelius Vanderbilt built the first Central Station up in the highlands near First (now Park) Avenue and 42nd Street in 1869 were silent now. However, smoke abatement was a critical concern, and city fathers ruled steam passenger trains would be outlawed in Manhattan after 1910 following a smoke-related train wreck that killed 17 in 1902. Meanwhile, rival railroad Pennsy was looking for a way to avoid using ferries to enter lower Manhattan. Both railroads chose to make use of recently-developed, electrically-operated train equipment and extensive tunneling.

For the PRR, the design contract was given to the firm of McKim, Mead & White, who used a combination of modern structural steel and classic building

70537 ELECTRIC LOCOMOTIVE IN PENNSYLVANIA STATION, NEW YORK.

run-through Pennsy facility, still-existent Grand Central actually features miles of track and underground loops below the city. There was a marshalling yard several miles away for even more equipment. In the day, it was heralded widely in the press for its stairless ramp-type walkways, clean layout, and wonderful amenities. Before it was finished in 1913, the wily Central sold or leased the 'air rights' above their property for a literal mint (still some of the most expensive real estate on the planet).

These two stations were fairly exclusive to the railroads that built them; the New Haven entered Grand Central as a partner, and PRR-affiliate Long Island Railroad came into Penn Station. The two structures were linked by New York's vast new subway system. The creation of the ill-fated Penn Central ended the need for separate facilities, though today both locations are still used for train movements. *

motifs for the design. This 28-acre Romanesque structure cost the line millions to build. At the time it opened in 1910, only the government itself had the equivalent resources to build something as large.

As planned, the station eliminated ferry trips. Passengers moved from steam-powered equipment to electric power at the newly-founded Manhattan Transfer depot in New Jersey, using tunnels under the Hudson to reach Manhattan. Further tunneling under the East River allowed trains to be turned in the huge Sunnyside Yard on Long Island. Times change, and Pennsylvania Station's shocking destruction in the mid-Sixties resulted in the widespread formation of today's historic preservation movement; its classic Post Office annex still survives.

As PRR construction continued downtown, arch-rival New York Central was also in the process of upgrading its Manhattan facilities with the new Grand Central Station several blocks away. Unlike the

Few postcards can equal the beauty shown in this reproduction of a Missouri Pacific painting by William H. Foster. This is the Sunshine Special, and its engine gave birth to the Pacific-type engine classification. The railroads spared little expense when promoting their best passenger services, and hiring highly-qualified illustrators like Foster was part of that effort.

In this day of four-hour flights between New York and Los Angeles and only four hours more to cross the ocean to Europe, it is hard to imagine a time when traveling itself was a vacation. For those crossing on water, the ultimate trips were via deluxe steamships that might take 10 days or more between destinations, and for those people crossing the continent, it was 'limited' rail service on the railroads.

The word 'limited' meant just that on a number of levels. The trains were limited in terms of accommodation (and clientele); only a select number of passengers would be given passage on the railroad's premiere consists on any trip. That service was surcharged over the normal point-to-point fare by as much as $25.00 (during the era when $25.00 was a good weekly wage). If demand and traffic warranted it, a 'second section' would be added. This would be an entirely separate train. In some cases, during busy periods such as holidays, the Santa Fe's **California Limited** and the New York Central's **20th Century Limited** ran in as many as seven sections, each separated only by the minimal safe distance needed between two fast trains.

They were also limited in terms of their stops; these limiteds were the trains that blasted through small towns on tight schedules. Their most celebrated clientele, mainly businessmen and entertainers, were on their own busy schedules which demanded, and received, excellence in speed and power. Many steam locomotive styles - the Pacific, the Hudson, the Northern - were developed for this level of high-speed service. This chapter will focus on the steam-powered consists that lasted from the turn of the century to the diesel era.

Pullman Service and Dining Experiences

Where these trains tried to be unlimited was in their willingness to meet every whimsy of their passengers. Though not a track owner, the huge Chicago-based Pullman Company owned many of these 'hotel on wheels' cars. Pullman cars first used beds converted from seating or stored above during the day. In later years, they also included special drawing rooms and 'roomette' bedrooms. They were furnished in rich woods and stained glass, and Pullman also staffed

The northeast region of the nation featured the largest concentration of rapid daylight trains. On the East Coast, day expresses like the Reading's Wall Street Special and the Lehigh Valley's Black Diamond vied with other lines for traffic into New York City. These two lines competed with the New York Central, Pennsylvania, Jersey Central, Long Island, Erie, and Delaware, Lackawanna & Western for passenger traffic.

For those desiring the historical approach to the Midwest, the B&O took a route along the aging canals of the Potomac before heading north toward Chicago from southern Ohio. The Capitol Limited was an all-Pullman consist, and was the line's premier train.

The Chicago & Alton issued a five-segment, multi-panel postcard of their fabled Alton Limited, which scorched the line's rails between Chicago and St. Louis. This is the mail/baggage combine.

these cars with men called porters, trained in the specifics of rail etiquette. The rest of the train would include a dining car with reservation-based service, lounge or club cars for before- and after-dinner refreshments, a smoking car for that gentleman who enjoyed a fine cigar (few 'ladies' of this era imbibed in the tobacco habit, and, if they did, it was not in public), and the train-ending observation car with an open platform or windowed view of the receding scene. There were varied special services offered as well, perhaps a barber or manicurist, a library or drawing room, areas set aside for business dictation, and special women's lounges. Each new innovation, from electric lights to showering rooms, was used with a flair for the dramatic in advertising and promotion.

Though the railroads did charge a premium for such services, the dining experience might actually cost them $0.50 on each dollar made; the important thing was to get passengers to remember their meal as a

A dining car kitchen on the Lehigh Valley in the pre-1907 era. Though space was small for the cook, he turned out great meals that were in turn served on china, silver, and linen finery in the adjoining dining area.

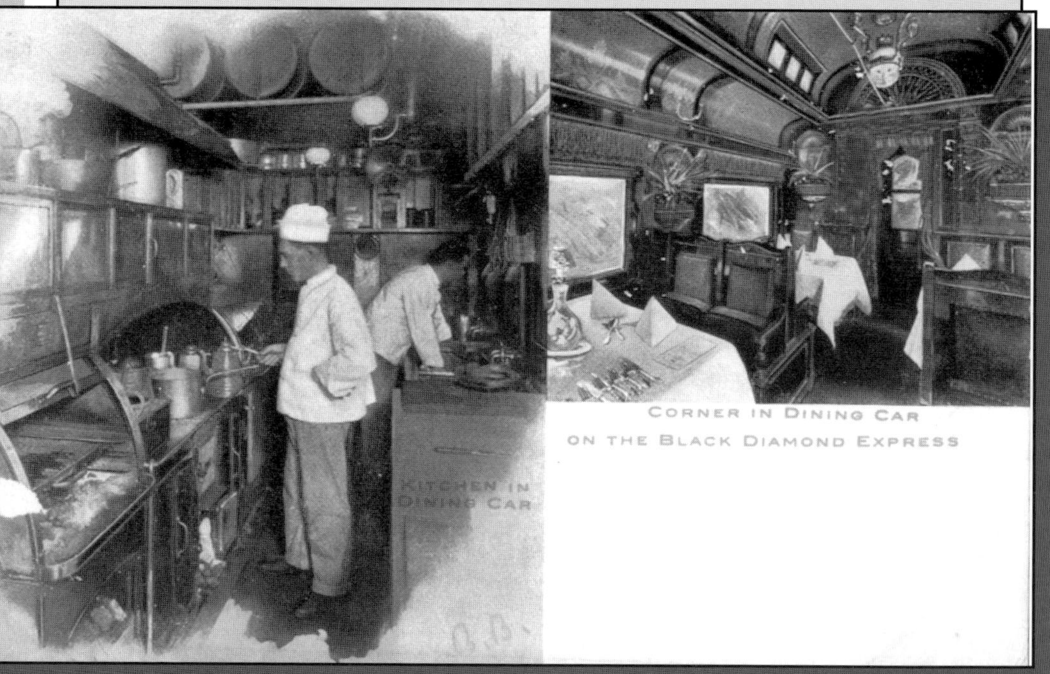

wonderful experience. In terms of fare, the rider could get fresh salmon when traveling to the Northwest, Maine lobster in New England, antelope steak on the Great Plains, and hush puppies in the Deep South. And all the while, the scene viewed through the car window changed, the premier train passing slower trains and factory works, mountain sides and rivers, speeding onward through day and night toward its destination.

The railroads promoted their 'limited' services as their premier offering; only the wealthiest patrons could do better, by owning or renting an entire rail car for personal use. The best overnight versions consisted of only Pullman cars, while many others consisted of coach-and-Pullman accommodations. Since some finished passage in a day, the limiteds could be broken down into four distinct categories: the daylight express, the lines east and west of Chicago, and the southern corridors.

Daylight Express Service

The daylight express was just as it sounds - a rapidly-moving limited that normally lasted only a portion of a day. These generally plied very well-traveled corridors that were also served by slower commuter trains. The Washington to Boston regions were the largest, followed by Chicago to either Milwaukee or St. Louis, then the Midwest (Detroit/

(right) The long tunnels and difficulty encountered running steam locomotion in the mountains led some lines across the Pacific Northwest region to be electrified. This Milwaukee Road card features the huge bi-polar electric engine that debuted in 1915, crossing the snowy heights with 'The Olympian,' the C.M. St. P. & P.'s premier train. This rare card, printed on thinner stock then most other postcards, is also unique in that it features a color company logo on the rear.

(left) This club car on the Burlington was a comfortable way to have a drink while the miles passed through the large windows on the left; the enclosed area to the right is the passageway through the train itself.

Vying for the transcontinental traffic was Union Pacific's **Overland Limited,** *seen here getting underway on a cold Wyoming day with a string of Pullman cars enroute to the California coast. The year: 1910.*

(right) Two railroads late to go the diesel route were the Norfolk & Western and the Wabash. These linen cards show their best-known passenger trains from the 1930s and 1940s; later, both of these limiteds would feature stream-lined or semi-streamlined steam engines.

PASSING THE PALISADES ALONG NEW RIVER IN VIRGINIA

WABASH "BANNER BLUE", ST. LOUIS - CHICAGO

Columbus/Indianapolis) hubs, and, to a much lesser extent, southern and western cities that were close enough together to warrant such service. Since these expresses competed between many larger cities, some of these routes would be among the earliest to go streamlined as covered in a later chapter.

It can be reasoned that the lines into New York supported the majority of the day expresses, moving bankers from Boston, business buyers from Baltimore, aldermen from Albany, and philanthropists from Philadelphia. The large number of railroads into the Big Apple meant the competition was steep between competing lines, particularly through New Jersey where so many ended with a ferry ride (occasionally replaced by taking the 'tubes' into Manhattan). The express trains

The '400' was the Chicago & North Western's entry into the battle for Chicago-St. Paul traffic. It was so named because it went the approximately 400 miles between the two cities in 400 minutes. This is a scarce linen postcard of the steam-powered version from the mid-1930s.

THE FAMOUS "400" SHOWN LEAVING THE CHICAGO STATION OF THE CHICAGO & NORTH WESTERN RAILWAY

THE TRAIN BETWEEN CHICAGO AND ST. PAUL - MINNEAPOLIS THAT SET THE PACE FOR THE WORLD

and their slower brethren on the New York Central, the Pennsylvania, the Reading, the Lackawanna, the Erie, the Jersey Central, and others were in fact responsible in many ways for the suburbs of New York, with high-paying jobs downtown less than an hour away from the gentle countryside.

Out of Chicago, competition for day passengers was just as fierce. Going north, the Chicago & North Western, Burlington Route, and Milwaukee Road battled for that traffic with trains that would top 90 mph or better on a daily basis, to both Milwaukee and Minneapolis / St. Paul. Several other lines, among them the New York Central, Illinois Central, and Wabash, used fast service to attract the same traffic going south through the Land of Lincoln to St. Louis. Of course, there were trains leaving the sprawling rail infrastructure of Chicago to points in every other direction as well. For example, there were day expresses to Louisville, Ky., and these trains also competed for traffic, especially during the spring rush to the Kentucky Derby.

Pullman Deluxe Overnight Trains

That the biggest battle for the overnight passenger was between New York and Chicago is not surprising. Though several lines such as the B&O and Erie also vied for this traffic, the two biggest rivals were the ***20th Century Limited*** of the New York Central (whose line was known as the Water Level Route), and the ***Broadway Limited*** of the Pennsylvania, named not for the city street but for the three- and four-abreast tracks along much of the route that it ran. These both debuted in 1902 with great fanfare, and through mutual consent, increased their respective speeds until the trip between the two locales was less than 16 hours long. Frankly, there is no comparison today to the level of sophistication and service that these trains offered in their glory years; numerous postcards documented their passing.

For longer trips across the west from the Windy City, the battle was between the transcontinental lines - the Atchison, Topeka & Santa Fe against the Union Pacific and Rock Island routes into California, and the Great Northern, Northern Pacific, and Milwaukee Road into the Pacific Northwest (via St. Paul). Postcards of these trains were often done as views or portraits showing the rugged terrain they covered.

The Pennsylvania Railroad may have fought the Allegheny Mountains in its namesake state, but those obstacles were inconveniences

Competing for identical clientele, the New York Central's 20th Century Limited *and the Pennsylvania's* Broadway Limited *were the final word in travel between New York and Chicago. Many cards were issued of these two trains, though some are quite rare and interior postcard views of this duo are almost unheard of. The Walter Greene painting image on the right was also used on a calendar in the 1920s.*

compared to what faced lines crossing the Rockies or Cascades between the Great Plains and the West Coast. Here tunneling for miles was sometimes required. Mountains and canyons needed extensive bridging and filling, and trackage clung to cliff-sides on shelves blasted clear by explosives. In the struggle against such natural obstacles, trains were sometimes powered by overhead electric lines. The Milwaukee Road in particular created numerous postcards of their electrification efforts through the Bitterroot Mountains of Montana.

Southern Living

As tourism grew in the new century, limited overnight service between both the Northeast and Midwest to the South became more prevalent. Many well-known limiteds in the South ran over a consortium of rail lines which expedited passengers day and night to the beaches of the Sunshine State. Each line treated these Pullman trains carried over its tracks as flagships. For example, the ***Silver Meteor*** was a streamlined train that ran over the Pennsy, RF&P, and Seaboard Air Line to reach between Miami and New York.

There were, of course, limiteds in many other regions of the nation, and postcards exist of many of them. In terms of demand, complete sets showing interior views are likely at the top of most collectors' lists. In some cases, the more obscure the line, the better. Single cards from these groups are also in demand. Next would be real photo cards showing these trains in service, followed in interest by those cards issued by the railroads themselves of the trains. Many of these cards were reproduced from the paintings that also appeared on the line's calendars and other printed matter. There are also localized views of the limiteds, often stating the train and the town through which it is passing.

The limited expresses were a dynamic and regular part of the landscape during the postcard craze; the broadest variety seems to come from the lines of the Northeast, where competition was the fiercest. There are a large number of white border cards from the 1920s in this category, but the linen era begun in the 1930s finds only a few. This is due to the Great Depression and its effects on advertising, plus the advent of streamlined diesels, which diminished some of the appeal of the mighty steam engine.						*

While a vast majority of the postcards produced over the years featured a single image, the advertising desires of some railroads led to cards that featured multiple images on a single standard-sized card, known as 'multi-view' cards. By no means considered commonplace during the postcard era, these cards are noteworthy in that they often display creative designs, lettering, and detail. Due to the time and expense involved, few businesses created and executed cards of this nature, though local publishers often adopted this format for scenes from a city, town, or region. Local real-photo postcard producers would also produce mulit-view cards on occasion (see p.122). The examples shown on this page give just an idea of the thought and execution of these cards, which are in demand today.

(above) **The Burlington Route** *and the* **Northern Pacific** *teamed up for this classic train, called the* **Northern Pacific Express** *westbound and the* **Atlantic Express** *when it came back east. This allowed the railroads to sell through tickets to the competitive Chicago-area market. Incidentally, no transcontinental trains went from coast to coast in this era.*

(above) **No expense was spared on the** Pioneer Limited *of the* Milwaukee Road, *which ran on the highly-competitive Chicago-St. Paul / Minneapolis corridor. As shown here, these trains featured lavishly-appointed interiors with rare finished woods, special lighting, and lead-glass windows. At this time, cars were still wooden with steel frames; Pullman would debut the first all-steel car in 1907.*

(left) **The Burlington** *advertised the benefits of its long-distance service that included the highlights of Colorado in the daytime. This train would be a fore-runner of the well-remembered* California Zephyr *of the streamlined era.*

The year was 1933, and newly-elected President Franklin D. Roosevelt was trying to bring the stalled economy of the United States back to life again. A pall hung over the nation's Depression-ridden businesses, and many of the biggest companies in railroading were either in bankruptcy or receivership. The Depression had hammered the rail industry at a time when it was already losing passenger traffic to planes and automobiles as well as freight movements to the growing interstate trucking industry. Nonetheless, it was in this era of financial despair that some of the most desirable railroad postcards came into being.

In Chicago, plans for that city's centennial had resulted in a giant exhibi-

(top) The trend-setting CB&Q Zephyr *was at the depot in* **Prairie du Chien, Wis. during its barnstorming tour in 1934. The early streamlined diesels and steam engines (New York Central's** Commodore Vanderbilt **seen at far left with 19th century** Dewitt Clinton*) **gave way to the colorful but standardized EMD-powered limiteds like the Great Northern's** Empire Builder *in the postwar era.*

tion called the 'Century of Progress.' Held right on the edge of Lake Michigan, this event has been heralded by some as a turning point in the 'Art Deco' movement's influence on the general populace. Streamlined design was being introduced to even the most utilitarian of items, and the buildings and displays at the event reflected this. As the city was a virtual hub of American railroading, many of the lines that served Chicago (and even some that did not) took part by displaying their best or oldest equipment at the fair. Like the Baltimore & Ohio's 'Fair of the Iron Horse' held in the previous decade, the rail displays showed some equipment in action and others in a static setting. As postcards were an easy and inexpensive item to present to visitors, the railroads printed up literally millions of them and many are considered common today, although a few from this event are considered hard to find.

The Streamliner Arrives

The fair continued into the following year, and had a new visitor on May 26, 1934. This train was the Chicago, Burlington & Quincy's brand-new *Zephyr*, which had just completed a blistering 78 mile-per-hour inaugural run from Denver. The stainless-steel, three-car train was not the first streamliner; credit for that goes to the Union Pacific. However, the *Zephyr*, powered by a Winton diesel engine, was the start of a great battle of one-upsmanship between the railroads. Though diesel locomotives had been used by railroads in the past (mostly as switching or one-car passenger units), this was their first use in a highly publicized setting.

Only weeks before, the Union Pacific had become the first to take advantage of using these 'super modern' articulated trainsets powered by internal combustion engines. Earlier in 1934, they had debuted the aluminum-bodied *M-10000*, which they simply called '*The Streamliner*.' Like the Zephyr, it too was part of this second year of the Century of Progress. Also a three-car experi-

NORTH	Morning Trip	Afternoon Trip	SOUTH	Morning Trip	Afternoon Trip
Lv. Chicago	8:00 am	4:00 pm	Lv. Minneapolis	8:00 am	4:00 pm
Ar. St. Paul	2:30 pm	10:29 pm	Lv. St. Paul	8:30 am	4:30 pm
Ar. Minneapolis	3:00 pm	10:59 pm	Ar. Chicago	3:00 pm	10:59 pm

ment, the **M-10000's** success was quickly followed by other streamliners on the UP, and it is these latter versions that show up most often on postcards. UP trainsets like the *City of Denver*, *City of Portland*, and *City of Los Angeles* were larger and more capable than the initial version (which itself became the *City of Salina*), and they were all depicted on cards throughout the era leading up to World War II.

Not that the Burlington Route had stopped at just one *Zephyr*, either. Indeed, soon the railroad had several of the stainless-steel serpents singing down the rails. Individualized postcards were done for many of these, and cards depicting the more regionalized editions such as the *Ozark State Zephyr* or *Silver Streak Zephyr* are harder to come by then those from the well-known *Denver Zephyr*. Both of the streamlined pioneers of 1934 have also shown up on locally-produced real photo postcards as they barnstormed across the continent before actually going into revenue service.

Not only were these trains popular with riders, but

Rivals New York Central and Pennsylvania used streamlined steam locomotives. The Hudson-powered Mercury (seen at top in a real photo card shot by Railroad Photographs) was a crack daylight train, while the huge S-1 Pennsy experimental spent its short career in passenger service as well (right). The PRR 6100 was first displayed at the 1939-1940 New York World's Fair as a moving display. Both trains were based in the Midwest virtually all of their careers. Above is the Reading's stainless steel Crusader, which ran between Philadelphia and Jersey City.

they were actually sometimes more economical to operate than steam locomotives. The other railroads around the country took notice of what these two were doing. By 1936, many railroad lines had begun to jump on the 'streamliner' bandwagon.

These included the Boston and Maine (who operated the ***Flying Yankee*** in conjunction with the Maine Central), the Gulf, Mobile & Northern's ***The Rebel***, Illinois Central's ***Green Diamond***, and the Baltimore & Ohio, who had the ***Royal Blue*** and ***Abraham Lincoln***. These and other railroads found that the diesels could now be run both reliably and profitably in long distance passenger service. The pioneering Electro-Motive Corporation, which became the EMD division of General Motors, and other diesel builders soon had their hands full with orders from both new customers and satisfied users.

The Hiawatha — NOTHING FASTER ON RAILS BETWEEN CHICAGO-MILWAUKEE AND ST. PAUL-MINNEAPOLIS

The Milwaukee Road, which extended from Indiana to Washington state, chose to power its high-speed Hiawatha trainsets first with streamlined steam engines (seen here passing Tomah, Wis. near 100 mph), and later used diesel power like the Alco DL109, seen here just prior to the second World War. The Hiawatha was born in the highly competitive Chicago-Milwaukee market, where speed was truly king. Like most of the streamliners, its financial success was due to new lightweight cars and modern, stylish amenities. The Milwaukee Road's combination of colorful paint, aero styling, and on-time performance made the Hiawatha a classic example of the genre in the 1930s.

Streamline trains built by the American Car & Foundry Co., Berwick, Pa.

At top - The Gulf, Mobile & Northern chose American Car & Foundry (ACF) to build the pair of daylight streamliners they nicknamed "The Rebels." When this line became the Gulf, Mobile & Ohio, they purchased a wide variety of diesels, including the Alco DL-type engine styled by designer Otto Kuhler on the eve of World War II (seen at left).

Streamlined Steam: A Last Stand for Performance

The development and success of the streamliners had resulted from the ability to create lighter trains and resultant higher speeds. Albeit briefly, the nation's big steam locomotive builders benefitted from the streamlined era as well. In this industry, change often came slowly, and despite the successes of the diesel-powered pioneers, many leaders in the railroad business were wary of moving away from tried-and-true steam locomotion. So instead of ante-ing up for the diesels, they chose instead to adopt or create stylized steam engines.

As a result, the Milwaukee Road actually chose a smaller, high horsepower locomotive (with a 4-4-2 wheel arrangement known as an Atlantic type) for the inaugural versions of their new Chicago-Milwaukee streamliners called the *Hiawathas.* Many other railroads followed this approach, creating or refitting special locomotives for their most important trains, although often using bigger equipment. As a result, the New York Central, the Pennsylvania, the Santa Fe, and many other lines eventually put streamlined steam engines in service on some of their largest passenger trains.

These postcards are highly desirable today for several reasons. The trains were around briefly; the start of World War II ended the use of metal for aesthetic purposes and some of the shrouded engines were difficult to work on. As a result, in many cases their stylized sheetmetal was pulled off for scrap. Also, the diesel age was indeed approaching. The transcontinental railroads were actively promoting these engines more than the steam engines - even streamlined steam engines - and the latest diesels were more often the subjects on postcards. In some cases, the streamlined steam engine was the work of the best industrial designers of the 'streamline era'- men like Raymond Loewy and Henry Dreyfuss - making the cards prime examples of this art. Postcard collectors and railfans alike are drawn to the Art Deco styling, making the cards very collectible.

The most common of these streamlined steam images were a group done for the Southern Pacific of their new **Daylight** train. In other cases, depending on the railroad, cards showing these steam trains can range from hard-to-find to next-to-impossible. A railroadiana or postcard collector seeking a certain train or engine from a favorite line may look for many years to find it, if it exists at all.

TAPROOM In The TAVERN-LUNCH COUNTER-LOUNGE CAR Of The NEW "400"—Insert, POPULAR LUNCH COUNTER

North Western's Famous Streamliner "400" Operates Daily Between Chicago and St. Paul-Minneapolis Via Milwaukee

The Chicago & North Western upgraded the 400 to streamlined diesel operation in 1939 in an effort to compete with the Burlington and Milwaukee Road for Chicago - St. Paul express traffic; the lounge featured classic Deco styling, and there was a half-moon shaped speedometer located above the bar shown here.

The Kansas City Southern got into the act with its Southern Belle streamliner, which debuted in 1940 with a million-dollar investment. Serving an eager public between Kansas City and New Orleans, the trains were a big hit right off the bat. The railroad even held a beauty contest for Miss Southern Belle as a publicity stunt, and issued the interior card shown above as part of a now-scarce folder of postcards.

By 1937, the Santa Fe had both streamlined steam, in the form of one steam locomotive known as the **Blue Goose,** and a string of hot LA-Chicago diesel-powered trains. Fiercely battling the Union Pacific for this traffic, the Santa Fe made it a point to promote their fleet of streamliners (see p.40-41). By this time in the streamliners evolution, the newest trains had become non-articulated, meaning that cars could be added and subtracted as needed, which had not been possible with some of the earlier designs. In addition to its passenger trains, the Santa Fe also became one of the first lines to use the GM Electro Motive Division's newly-designed 'FT' multiple-unit diesel engine in freight service prior to the advent of World War II. Both types of trains show up on postcards given to servicemen traveling to and from the Pacific and Atlantic war theaters on Santa Fe's trains (see p.46). The EMD-designed graphics on the Santa Fe locomotives - a catchy red, yellow and silver design known as 'the Warbonnet'- shows up on millions of postcards. Nonetheless, they are popular among collectors.

Railroad Fairs and a Big War

The Century of Progress would not be the end of the World's Fair movement of the 1930s. The San Francisco Golden Gate Exposition and New York World's Fair at the end of the decade drew immense crowds during the final years before the war. Though the New York version had a Railroad Hall as well as a Railroads on Parade show, only a slight number of postcards were generated from this event other than ones of the building itself. Likewise, though railroads had a presence at the West Coast event, only a few cards exist. One linen

The Bar is the "refreshing" section of the beautiful lounge-observation car

Going south out of Chicago, the flagship train was the overnight **City of Miami** *on the Illinois Central, running between Chicago and Florida. Inaugurated in 1940, it left Chicago in the morning and put travelers into Miami the following afternoon. Passengers are enjoying a drink in the Florida-themed* **Bamboo Grove** *lounge-observation, which featured a special track map that illuminated the train's location as it traveled through the deep South.*

card was of a special Santa Fe steam train called the *Valley Flyer*. Serving the fair, this colorful outfit operated for only five months.

The 1940s and wartime demands brought business back to the railroads in immense quantity, though there are not many postcards specifically from that four-year period. The Pennsylvania and Santa Fe did cards for servicemen, and there are a number of releases from other railroads. However, the pressing needs of the nation did not bode well for recreational travel. New equipment was acquired on an as-need basis, and in some cases, completed equipment was actually sold to a critically-important railroad instead of the original buyer. Most travel postcards tended to be carryovers from the prewar era. The Frisco created a 10-card set that featured new engines, cars and services that likely appeared in the early 1940s as hostilities got underway.

Postwar Pluses and Minuses

When the war ended, the railroads found themselves in the enviable position of finally having some capital, which was much needed. The heavy traffic of the 1941-1945 era had taken its toll on equipment already worn out by the Depression era's deferred maintenance programs. As a result, major investments were being made across the nation to upgrade service for the postwar customer.

The companies that had been the prime movers in steam locomotive production - Baldwin, American (Alco), and Lima - found themselves playing second-fiddle to EMD's (Electro Motive Division) crack marketing and styling team, which had General Motors' resources behind it. The war had proven beyond a shadow of a doubt that the steam engine's days were indeed numbered, and even the biggest coal producers like the Pennsylvania and the Chesapeake & Ohio began putting in orders for machines that the engineers referred to as 'growlers.' However, the 'old guard' engine builders did have customer loyalty on their side and they produced a few diesel designs. These were somewhat short-lived, and postcards showing engines like Alco's DL-109 engine are not often seen. Though Alco would be the 'survivor' of the steam group and would produce some classic designs into the 1950s, EMD virtually controlled the postwar locomotive market.

The postcard business was changing as well. The color linen cards that made a sort of 'dreamscape' out of ordinary things during the early days of streamlining gave way to more realistic color photographs, called 'chromes' today. Introduced just prior to the war, these postcards (which did not need colorizing or retouching) became more popular as the decade of the Fifties began. Some of the early chromes done by the railroads are harder to come by than similar linen cards, but these are not in demand.

The decade of the Forties ended with the last big rail celebration of the steam era, the Chicago Railroad Fair. Many railroads participated in this, showing off their latest equipment. The Union Pacific's gigantic 1944-built steam engine, called the **Big Boy**, was featured on a special black-and-white litho card, as were several other trains. It would be steam's last hurrah, however, as the companies were retiring the locomotives, even newer ones, as quickly as the diesel builders could turn out internal combustion equipment. Several commemorative cards were done during the 1949-1953 period as certain rail-

Here the Wabash Railroad's City of Kansas City, *hammers out of its namesake town toward St. Louis, where customers could move over to the flagship* Blue Bird *for points north. Like many lines, the Wabash chose to upgrade its streamliners with the profits from the war years; it was one of the final lines to go the streamliner route, doing so in 1950.*

When traveling out into the West, rival lines Santa Fe and Union Pacific featured the latest equipment and a variety of possible accommodations. The **Overland Limited** *was replaced by the new "City" trains that traversed the famed transcontinental line from Omaha to California. The* **Challenger,** *whose diner is shown here, was introduced in 1937 and ran until 1947 when it was assimilated into other UP consists.*

roads like the Burlington, Illinois Central, and Rock Island celebrated their 100th Anniversaries.

Interest in linen postcards produced of the first and second generation streamliners continues unabated. Some versions have become truly rare, and, like images showing the small town depot, these cards are in solid demand nationwide.

The postwar era brought about many changes in American society. However, the freedom of better highways and commercial air travel would erode what remained of the classic passenger age in railroading. Moreover, Washington's regulatory requirements from the turn of the century would put the railroads at a disadvantage in the shipping business. The prosperity of the war years was brief. The Fifties would spell the 'last hurrah' for most of America's name trains - and the postcards associated with them.   *

H-2066 CAJON PASS AT THE SUMMIT OF THE COAST RANGE, CALIFORNIA

An entire book could be written on Fred Harvey's involvement with the Santa Fe Railway. Harvey, an Englishman by birth, revolutionized rail travel at the end of the 19th century by offering high-quality dining and overnight lodging services to rail patrons. Working in close association with the railroad, Harvey took over a run-down beanery in the Santa Fe's depot in Topeka, Kansas in the late 1870s, and by 1883 had taken over operation of every restaurant and hotel associated with the line. This string of on-line dining and lodging establishments was noted for their attractive, young and morally-upright women, known as Harvey Girls, ladies who became the subject of many poems, songs, and productions. Since he also operated various concessions for the railroad both on and off the trains, nearly all of the postcards from Santa Fe have Fred Harvey's name and logo on the back.

Actually, the Fred Harvey cards stretch across the divided back postcard era, although Harvey himself had died in 1901. The earliest railroad cards featured some of the immense engines the Santa Fe built (this railroad's 'super Mallet' of 1911 featured a 2-10-10-2 wheel arrangement, still one of the largest the world has ever seen) as well as scenes from the railroad. Harvey's colorful cards opened up

H-4510— THE "SUPER CHIEF," SANTA FE'S TRANSCONTINENTAL FLYER

H-4511—ONE OF THE DINING CARS ON THE SANTA FE'S "SUPER CHIEF"

the Western vistas to potential travellers. Many were done by Detroit Publishing Company during that firm's heyday as one of the premier postcard printers in North America. In addition to railroading, other Harvey cards focused on the national parks and Native American peoples.

However, the dawn of the streamlined age brought about even more fame for this storied railroad. With the advent of diesel power and the new **Super Chief** in 1936, most of the linen postcards done by Harvey featured these latest engines with the highly popular 'war-bonnet' paint scheme. These postcards are very common today and were done in literally dozens of different locales - in canyons, on bridges, at stations and, most commonly, entering orange groves on the last leg of the trip to California. Collectors should note, however, that many of the reissues done of these cards over the years suffer from heavy-handed retouching, which can negatively impact their values. This is true of all highly-retouched railroad subjects.

Interestingly, the Santa Fe's lone streamlined steam engine, a 4-6-4 Hudson type known as the **Blue Goose**, has been found only on two black-and-white Santa Fe Railway (not Harvey) issued postcards from the late 1930s era; both appear to be from a location in the line's Chicago yards (one is shown above right). Perhaps the need to publicize this machine did not interest the railroad; the scarce cards, however, are desired by both postcard and railroad aficionados today.

Like many railroads, there are some interior postcards of newly-introduced and unique equipment that are not easy to find today, although there are probably more Fred Harvey interiors examples on the market than other similar linen postcards. The interior design on the Santa Fe maintained a unique Southwestern motif (famed architect Mary Colter was among those who helped create this image).

The postwar era found the various **Chief** trains on postcards, and Fred Harvey cards and sets from the chrome period remain in abundance, although some are more desirable simply because they are more graphically pleasing. The 1960's decline in passenger service saw these cards disappear, although Amtrak continued to run some of the name Santa Fe trains after 1971. A Santa Fe postcard collector who desires a complete run of the Fred Harvey issues will find this a true challenge. One final note would be that complete sets including the unique Fred Harvey postcard set envelope (which featured several artistic cover designs over the years) are somewhat more desirable than single cards to the Harvey or Santa Fe collector.

*

In a simpler time, before television and personal computers, attending a large regional or national fair could have been the highlight of one's year. The railroads were involved with such events from the middle to late 1800s, and some went on to actually host 'railroad fairs' themselves. For the railroad enthusiast, it was a wonderful event. Shown here is a selection of the many railroad-issued postcards that made their appearances at a few of the events held between 1909 and 1949.

1939-1940 New York Worlds Fair
Few railroad cards were released from this New York event, though many famous engines were on display there. This view of the operating DeWitt Clinton is the best-known.

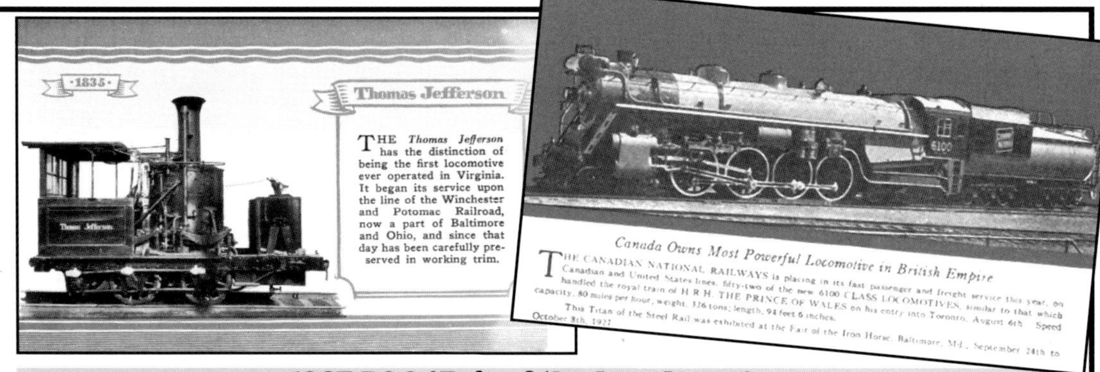

1927 B&O 'Fair of the Iron Horse'
The Baltimore & Ohio's 'Fair of the Iron Horse' was held at the Howard County, Maryland, Fairgrounds outside of the line's namesake city in 1927. In addition to a set of 15 cards issued by the railroad showing its own historical and modern equipment, a handful of other lines also displayed engines and had postcards available. Shown here with two B&O set issues is a card of the newest Canadian National engine from this event (above right).

1939 San Francisco Worlds Fair

Another huge event took place on the west coast on the eve of World War II, held in San Francisco during the summer of 1939. A handful of railroads had equipment on display, but postcards from this event were primarily of the entrance marques.

In 1832, the C. & O. Canal and the B. & O. Railroad struggled for the right-of-way along the Potomac near Harper's Ferry. In the resulting agreement the Railroad consented to build a "tight board fence" between railroad and canal to protect the horses from the engines
BALTIMORE AND OHIO RAILROAD
At "A Century Of Progress," Chicago, 1933

BURLINGTON ZEPHYR AT A CENTURY OF PROGRESS EXPOSITION — 1934
Built of stainless steel — Electric shot-welded — Rides on articulated trucks. Powered by an eight-cylinder, two-cycle, 660 horse-power, oil-burning Diesel engine. Runs on roller-bearings — Air-conditioned — Equipped for radio reception.

No. 1909, the "BIG MALLET" and No. 1, the "WILLIAM CROOKS"
On exhibition at the Alaska-Yukon-Pacific Exposition, Seattle. The largest engine used on the Great Northern Railway and its diminutive prototype. Average load capacity of the "Wm. Crooks" on a 1 per cent Grade 60 tons; that of the "Big Mallet" 1600 tons. The "Big Mallet" hauls practically as much tonnage as twenty-five "Wm. Crooks". No. 1909, the "BIG MALLET" [Built in 1908] Weight on drivers 355,000 lbs. Total weight, engine and tender 530,200 lbs. Diameter of driving wheels 55 ins. 4 cylinders. 2 high pressure 22½ ins. 2 low pressure, 33 ins. by 32 ins. No. 1, the "WILLIAM CROOKS" [Built in 1861] Weight on drivers 55,400 lbs. diameter of driving wheels 63 ins. 1 cylinder. 12 ins. by 22 ins.

1933-34 Chicago Century of Progress

The big fair that took place during the Great Depression in Chicago found several railroads giving cards away. These included local lines like the Burlington, which featured an on-site Railway Post Office car (and whose issues are the most common), the Milwaukee Road, and the Chicago & North Western, as well as displaced lines like the Delaware & Hudson, and Nashville, Chattanooga & St. Louis. The B&O also issued a set of 14 postcards for this occasion, one which is featured above left.

A rare Great Northern card from the 1909 Alaska-Yukon-Pacific Exposition in Seattle.

In the foreground is the Minnetonka, Northern Pacific Railway's first locomotive as it appeared in "Wheels A-Rolling," Chicago Railroad Fair pageant of transportation progress. The Minnetonka, built in 1870, is 27 ½ feet long, 10 feet 2 inches high, weighs 12 tons and costs $6,700. In comparison, the new 4500 H. P. Diesel locomotives which power the streamlined North Coast Limited are 151 feet 4 inches long, 15 feet high, weigh 345 tons and cost $458,000. The headend of one of the Diesels is shown in the background.
PRINTED IN U. S. A.

1948-1949 Chicago Railroad Fair

As the postwar era got underway in earnest, the railroads pulled out all the stops one last time for a huge operating display at the site of the 1933 Century of Progress event. Numerous lines took part in this two-year extravaganza, and cards

showing trains were issued by the Northern Pacific, Pennsylvania, Union Pacific, and Burlington, among others. Though often common, collecting an entire series from the events shown here can be quite challenging.

STEAM, STEEL & SUCCESS

2392 View at the Hanna Docks, Ashtabula, Ohio.

The railroad's involvement in the steel process began at two points of origin - the ore fields of the upper Midwest, and the coal fields of the eastern United States. Coal and its byproduct coke were both required to turn the raw ore into the final product, so while northern lines were hauling heavy red earth towards the cavernous Great Lakes freight ships, the eastern roads were bringing in tons of coal to feed the blast furnaces from the opposite direction. In fact, the ships arriving with ore would return north full of coal in some instances.

Once a ship had arrived at a place like Ashtabula or Huron, Ohio, huge cranes that could quickly scoop out tons of ore at a time would be put into service unloading it. The ore would be weighed and put into waiting rail cars. Some cars were specialized for the service, while others had come west filled with coal. Then, depending upon the rail line, multiple engines would struggle to bring the ore east, originally to the early processing plants like the example shown at Genesee, New York. These small operations gave way to the huge sprawling mills, or "works," in places like Youngstown, Ohio, and Pittsburgh, Allentown, and Bethlehem, Pa.

There, the process of refining the material into steel would result in fresh rail, tube stock, or rolled steel sheets, virtually all of which would be again loaded onto rail cars for shipment to the manufacturing sector. Automobile plants, appliance factories, stamping plants and foundries, and construction firms were among the many businesses that used the railroads to bring material in. Then, more often than not, they used the railroads again to take the finished product on to its final retail destination.

Times changed, and the great steel rush is no longer part of the nation's industrial might. The cranes of northern Ohio are gone now, as are most of the steel mills themselves. As one might imagine, postcards that illustrated this business are in demand. They are sought after by collectors who pursue images of the steel industry, by railroad collectors, and by regional collectors, most of whom share a sense of strange melancholy about this particular demise of the nation's industrial heritage. ✳

ON THESE PAGES - From upper left top - Ore is moving from the red iron fields of Hibbling, Minn. toward Lake Superior ships and the hearths of the Midwest (1910), while a strip-mining crane is digging coal from the anthracite-rich region of Hazleton, Pa. (1925). Coal also came from mines located all along the Alleghany range, such as this small operation in Leechburg, Pa. (1910). (far left) The large image of the unloading cranes at work at the Pennsylvania Railroad's sprawling operation in Ashtabula, Ohio is also shown in detail above (1910, 1920). To get the ore to the mills required big power; the Bessemer Railroad had Baldwin build the world's largest Consolidations to leave Conneaut, Ohio, which ran in push-pull fashion as seen here (1909). Ore and coal ended up in big mills like Republic's works in Youngstown, Ohio (1935) or small operations like the Genesee (N.Y.) blast furnace (1905). Ready availabililty of rolled steel helped Willys-Overland ship 1,000 cars a day from their Toledo, Ohio plant over the New York Central (1920).

While a majority of the railroad postcards produced over the years focused on passenger service and equipment, most of the business of railroading itself was based on moving freight. Throughout North America, railroads served businesses ranging from the local farm co-op or feed mill to the largest manufacturing plants and facilities. From the end of the horse-drawn age until the dawn of the interstate highway system, there were few alternatives to the railroad companies when it came to shipping, a monopoly which eventually resulted in legislation during the Progressive era that set fixed rates for most rail-based services. This also led to the establishment of the Interstate Commerce Commission, which regulated the industry through much of the postcard era.

But for enthusiasts of railroading, none of that political intrigue and industrial frustration is really important. For them, the lonesome sound of a steam whistle echoing through the night, the weaving of heavy-laden cars descend-

The epoch movement of American postwar freight is shown here. Steam's final years of glory were highlighted by new engines on the Frisco (St. Louis-San Francisco) during World War II (seen at left) and the big M-class Challengers of the Western Maryland passing each other in an issue from the 1951 York Interstate Fair (at top), with both cards focused on freight service. Above is a Santa Fe Railway card distributed to American troops during the Second World War. The FT-style diesels built by EMD on this refrigerated freight consist marked the coming internal combustion revolution. The FT locomotive was the true beginning of the rapid demise of steam locomotion once hostilities were over.

ing a grade with roars and squeals and brake smoke swirling around behind, or the clickity-clack monotony of a mile-long string of steel wheels passing over rail joints at every 40-foot interval were the stuff of hobo-ing dreams and big business in motion. Though trains still run today, most of these sights and sounds are history.

Business as Usual

The railroad freight business overall was often filled with interchange and speed. Refrigerated traffic in the steam age might leave southern California or Florida or Washington state and be expedited through three or more rail systems on its way to New York or Detroit or Chicago only days later, stopping only to change crews or engines and to drop large cakes of melting ice through the 'reefer' car's roof-mounted hatches. An automobile manufacturer might send four or five boxcar-loads of new vehicles from their plant each day, heading to different destinations nationwide. A heavy coal train might work its way slowly through the mountains to the ocean shore for export via ship,

Fast fruit is highlighted in these corporate art renderings. At top, one of the Seaboard's trains of oranges heads north through the Florida groves. Above, the Union Pacific issued this card of Washington State showing apple orchards as part of a series of artworks from each of the states it traversed. Refrigerated traffic is still a serious part of modern railroading.

while a cattle train might race its way from the plains of Nebraska to the sprawling stock yards in Kansas City or Omaha with baying livestock.

In between the points of origination and destination, these cars would be tracked using an extensive paper trail and placed into specific trains based on the need for speed. For example, the fastest freight train leaving St. Louis for Detroit overnight might have a dozen of those West Coast produce refrigerated cars, plus another half dozen reefer cars filled with bananas from a port at New Orleans, Florida produce, and meats from Kansas City. There could be box cars serving the auto industry with parts for vehicle construction, tank loads of chemicals coming up from Texas or Louisiana for the same purpose, or any number of other products that needed to be in the Motor City before the next day.

Each railroad in the process would use different levels of importance (perishables, dry goods, bulk loads) to determine which shipment arriving in their yard might go out in a couple of hours, and which one might sit for a day or more. So while our fast train heads north non-stop, a slower regular freight train might be stopping a few times on its trip to Detroit. This train might have coal hoppers or boxcars, some empty and

some full, plus other cars to be dropped off at various yards along the route. Those cars would be sorted by final business location, and either sent on to the next railroad or to their final destination in local, or 'peddler,' freight trains. These same trains would also gather other cars as they went about their work, which would be sent back to the yard to be picked up by our hypothetical train returning toward St. Louis the following day. From there, the process would start all over again.

Freight Train Postcards

For postcard collectors, freight train examples cover a variety of images and uses. For example, a railroad, the shipper, or a local postcard producer might create a card denoting a large or unique movement of a single product - 'a mile-long string of....'- whatever. However, documenting special movements like this were a fairly uncommon occurrence. Much more likely would be a generic image of a train moving through a certain type of terrain or setting, such as climbing up a mountain pass or crossing a bridge or trestle. Since the railroads themselves would normally use passenger trains for these types of images, most of those cards showing freight train movements of this sort were done by a local firm.

In another type of card, the railroad or local publisher might choose to use the postcard medium to depict the latest in freight motive power. This was particularly prevalent as the Mallet-type steam locomotives (those having two individual sets of larger driving wheels) grew in size from the late 1890s until the 1920s. As this evolution continued, many railroads laid hold of the term 'world's largest locomotive,' which it may indeed have been…for a week or a month until an even larger example debuted. Later, horsepower changes were often based more on efficiency then on sheer dimensions. It should also be noted that by the 1920s, the popularity of postcards had

Above -This early 1900s view shows a big, non-compound, single-cylinder, articulated Great Northern steam engine in Hillyard, Washington's rail yards. At top, one of the Union Pacific "Big Boy" 4000-class steam engines is pulling a mile of cars up over Sherman Hill outside of Cheyenne, Wyo., in a regional postcard from the 1950s; this is the line's best-remembered PR photo of these locomotives.

Caboose postcards are somewhat unique; this is one of a modern (for its day) Erie Railroad bay window caboose published in the 1970s by Audio-Visual Designs. The photo itself was likely 20 years old by then, and could have been taken as part of the railroad's 1951 Centennial.

lost its fad status, which helps account for fewer cards of gargantuan freight motive power after that date.

The interest in these cards can be driven by card type and rarity (such as a real photo of a new engine at rest or in service from a seldom-documented line), card quality, and locomotive design. The Virginian Railway and the Erie Railroad both attempted locomotives that had three sets of driving wheels for their heavy grades, hoping to alleviate the need for double or triple (or more) engines on a single train. Postcards of these experiments would be of interest to collectors of those lines or of locomotive history. The larger engines depicted on many postcards were compound styles, using steam twice. The steam was used first in a set of small, upper cylinders, then through a set of larger, lower cylinders, before being exhausted

Moving freight might require a steam boat ride for the cars, as seen in this rare card of the Chattanooga, Nashville & St. Louis's operation at Gunterville, Alabama, or simply dumping into the hull of a ship, like the Norfolk and Western did at Newport News, Va.

Logging was one industry that rarely interchanged cars, whether they be the standard gauge versions shown fully loaded on the Wenachee Valley & Northern in Washington state, or on the narrow gauge at Tuolumne, California. The railhead normally ended at a lumber mill, and finished products would be what headed out to the mainline rails.

through the stack atop the boiler. The earlier versions have just one large pair of cylinders to drive the wheels. These sluggers were built for power, not for speed. In most opinions, the largest, most efficient freight steam engine was the Union Pacific's 4000-class **Big Boy**, a compound Mallet which was created during the Second World War in steam construction's twilight years.

Toward the end of the passenger era, some railroads began to use postcards to promote their role in providing freight service to the general public. The dawn of the freight diesel era saw some railroad-issued postcards created in the interest of showing the public that the said railroad was more 'modern' than its competitors. Others, notably the Western Maryland's 1951 York (Pa.) Interstate Fair issues, depicted both the latest diesels and some steam power. As mentioned in the corporate photography section starting on page 80, some of the cards done feature matched sets of the line's newest freight cars, especially when those cars were for special or high-speed service.

The next type of freight-oriented postcard might showcase trains in action at a particular industrial location. Such places would include ship yards and docks, mines of various sorts, refineries, mills, etc. Usually, this style of card was an overview of a business or operation as opposed to something done by the railroad; the trains were simply part of the industrial landscape. Postcards of this sort are not overly rare. Birds-eye type overviews would be considered the most common, while real-photo images in sharp focus would be considered the most important. In some instances, the image may be showing freight being transshipped from railcar to wagon or ship, or visa versa. These postcards will appeal to a variety of collectors interested in either the style of industry shown, the locale itself , or the transportation forms depicted. As mentioned in the Art & Artists chapter, industrial paintings by artist Howard Fogg are quite prolific on postcards from the 1960s era.

Another, somewhat-hard-to-come-by style of card may depict a singular car for the purpose of advertising or promotion. These cards include refrigerated beer boxcars (especially from the pre-Prohibition era), special tank cars, special cars used for oversize or heavy-weight shipping, and specially-painted cars, among others. One such example would be the red-white-and-blue 'State of Maine' mechanically-refrig-

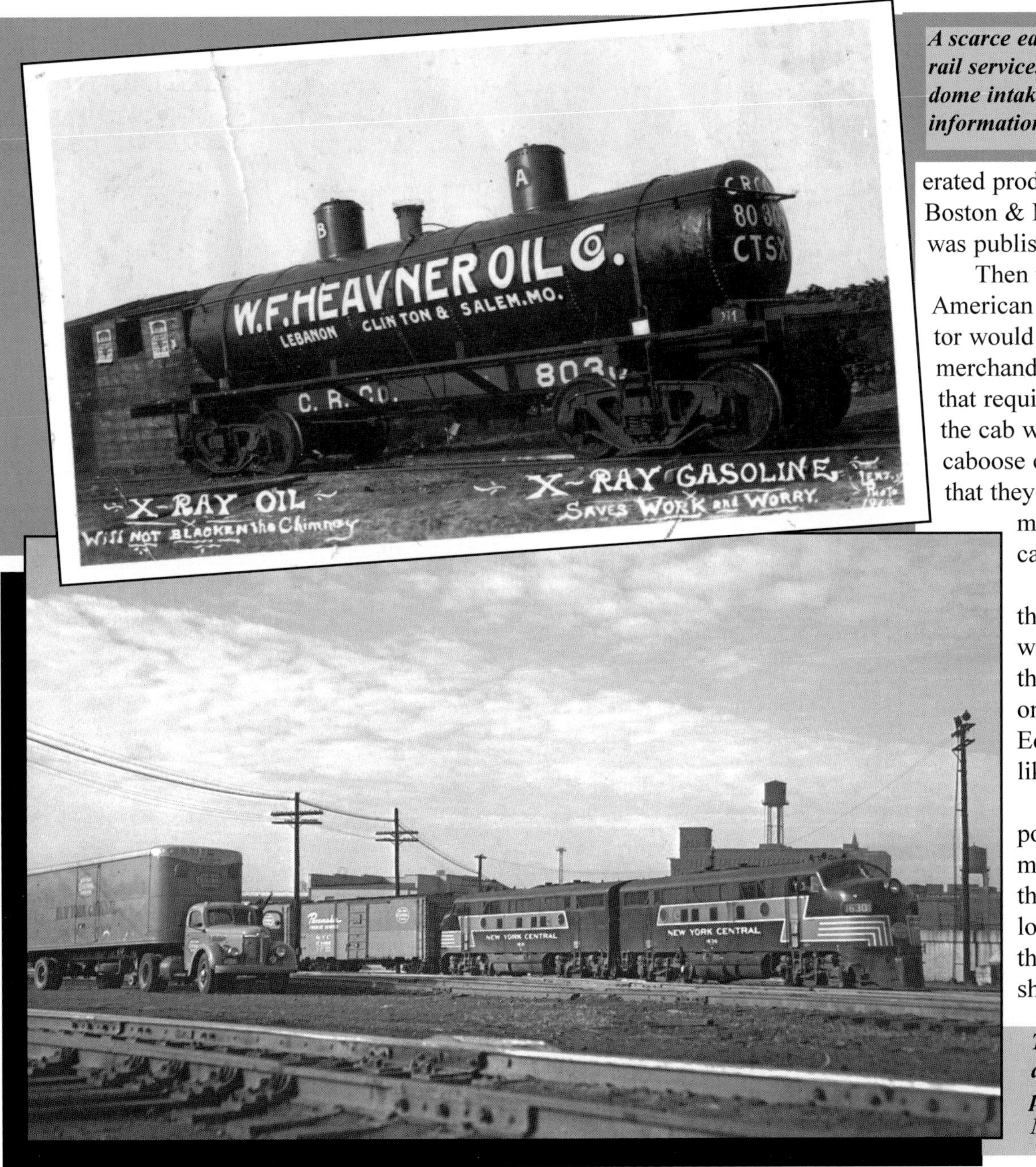

erated product pool boxcars used by the Bangor & Aroostook or Boston & Maine. A chrome-type postcard showing this colorful car was published in the 1950s by these railroads.

Then there was the caboose. Now largely displaced from the American scene, this was the office of the train, where the conductor would take care of the management of the rail cars and the merchandise in them under his control. Today, only those trains that require them by law regularly use cabooses; the crew rides in the cab with the engineer. While there is no noted subcategory of caboose collectors, they appear infrequently enough on postcards that they should be considered somewhat unique. A few cards, mostly chromes from the post-1960 era, even feature caboose images as a primary subject.

Rounding out the freight postcards would be the ones that show oversize produce or products in a humorous way. There were several producers of these, and other than the 'larger than life' real photo cards, they tend to have only novelty significance. Some of the early cards done by Edward Mitchell in this genre remain available in mint or like-new condition on the secondary postcard market.

Today's freight trains are occasionally documented on postcards from the makers of modern railfan cards. For most collectors, however, the period best recalled and in the most demand was headed up by a hard-working steam locomotive and ended with a rolling caboose…which, in the minds of many enthusiasts, was well how the world should be.

*

One of the outstanding features of the Bridgton region is the Bridgton-Harrison Railway. The line is unusual in using a track gauge of only two feet and is the only common carrier of its kind in the country still in operation.

While Maine had its share of full size railroads like the Maine Central, represented here by locomotive #510, train enthusiasts of a narrow gauge persuasion were taken in by the likes of Bridgeton & Saco River #5 at Hiram (later Bridgton Junction); this postcard of an Ed Bond photo was done as a book promotion in the 1960s. (black-and-white uncoated stock)

By the end in 1940, the Bridgeton & Harrison line was being promoted as a scenic way to get to the resorts of Rangeley Lake; as the 24" trains were disappearing, several railfan groups chartered excursions on the lines. (linen 1940s)

Like the Colorado lines, the Bridgeton & Harrison found converting motor cars for rail use was an economical way to deal with dwindling passenger and freight revenues. (litho 1930s)

Engine #7 in service at the Edaville, Mass., cranberry farm, which kept the Maine 24" equipment from being completely scrapped. (chrome 1940s)

The inadequate building standards common to most narrow gauge lines often led to scenes like this Maine bridge collapse in 1905 on the Waterville, Wicasset & Farmington. (color litho 1900s)

A ticket from the Bridgeton & Saco River circa 1920s

The depots of the Maine narrow gauge lines remain among the most popular and evasive for the postcard collector. This was Farmington on the Sandy River & Rangeley Lakes in about 1915; the 24" trackage is going across the card from the left.

330 North from Summit of Mt. McClellan, Argentine Central Ry. Colorado.

6734   HIGH BRIDGE, GEORGETOWN LOOP, COLO.

7219   Ophir Loop near Telluride, Colo.

DETROIT PUBLISHING Co.

Deep in the fabric of the history of railroading in America is a group of diminutive railways built to a track gauge smaller than the standard 4' 8" rail-to-rail width. Ranging from 24" to 36" inches in gauge, these commercial lines serving the public were originally built beginning in the latter part of the 1800s. with economy of construction and operation in mind. They were particularly popular in areas where mountains and other natural obstacles greatly increased the cost of standard gauge railroad construction. Their chief downside was the fact that the narrow-gauged cars could not be interchanged with other, wider-gauge rail lines. Any materials carried had to be transferred over to standard gauge cars at the narrow gauge line's terminus. However, with raw materials like precious ores, coal, or timber, this was not an issue because refining, sorting, or treatment of those products was often done at the same location as transfer.

By the dawn of the 20th Century and the beginning of the picture postcard era, those narrow-gauge rail lines that had not been reconstructed to the standard rail width were at their zenith. Nonetheless, conversion to standard gauge was already quickly moving forward for any railroad that required direct interchange of cars for survival. Those that didn't convert generally failed and were gone by the quarter-century mark with few exceptions.

On small tourist-oriented lines like the Revere Beach in Massachusetts, and in the logging industry nationwide, narrow gauge

As lines went to standard gauge, narrow gauge operations in many locales included dual-gauge trackage such as seen here in the famous Royal Gorge of Colorado; the train itself in this image is standard 4'-8" gauge. The outside right-hand rail and the rail in the center were used by 36" gauge trains.

Among the tourist attractions that help make Colorado's narrow gauge lines famous were the Georgetown loop (top) on the Colorado & Southern, the summit of Mount McCellen of the Argentine Central, and the trestles at the mining area of Ophir on the Rio Grande Southern. These railroads maintain a strong hobbyist following to this day.

held sway since there was little need to change. These operations did virtually no direct interchange with other railroads. In Pennsylvania, one line that was primarily a coal hauler, the East Broad Top, made use of an overhead crane to lift and convert standard gauge rail cars to a 36" wheelset, an ingenuity which helped it to survive into the 1950s.

Others remained as narrow gauges based on their locale. Until the 1950s, the Southern Pacific maintained a narrow gauge branch between Keeler, California, and the gold town of Tonopah, Nevada, which was lightly trafficked. The same was true of an isolated

Birdseye View of Santa Cruz, Cal.

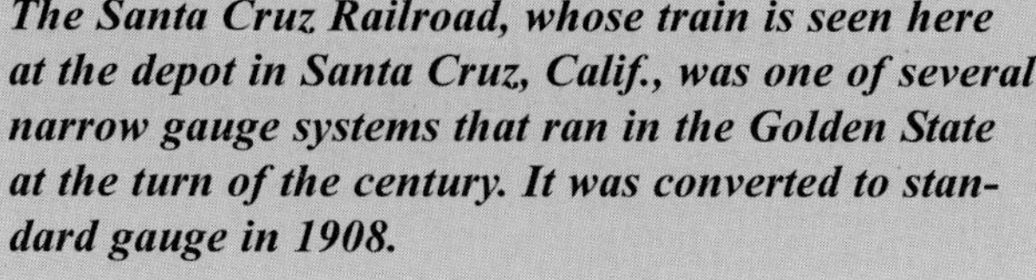

Pennsylvania Railroad subsidiary, the Waynesburg & Washington, which was not converted to standard gauge until 1943. Another good example would be the East Tennessee & Western North Carolina, which served the hill people between Johnson City, Tenn. and Boone, N.C., during the first half of the Twentieth Century. After flood damage took out part of its route in 1940, it survived another decade in shortened form, finally converting what remained profitable to standard gauge in 1950. The White Pass & Yukon in Alaska, isolated almost completely from interchange, was one North American line that actually purchased and operated narrow-gauge diesel power following the Second World War.

And then there were the states of Colorado and Maine…

The state of Colorado remains the true mecca of American narrow gauge railroading. The terrain of the Rocky Mountains coupled with the vital need to move gold and silver ores from remote areas to the Front Range cities like Denver and Pueblo made the state a natural for narrow gauge development, which had its apex of popularity just as the major gold strikes were being made. So, over snowy passes and through dark canyons, agile 36" gauge trains soon made their way into hidden places like Black Hawk, Leadville, Silverton, and Ophir, quick-

Showing its years is Southern Pacific locomtive #18 at Keeler, Calif., in 1952. Due to the low traffic density of the area, the railroad saw no need to make this Mojave desert branch line a standard gauge operation. They eventually abandoned it in favor of truck service.

ly earning a large return on their investment as they moved raw ores from mine to smelter and on to the mints. They also paced through some of the most rugged and beautiful scenery in North America, sometimes gaining elevation by looping over their own rails; a number of these railroads interconnected to form the now-legendary "Narrow Gauge Circle."

Though standard gauge quickly became prevalent throughout the rest of the nation, much of the Centennial State remained served by narrow-gauge trains, whose wholesale conversion to wider, heavier usage was cost-prohibitive. Indeed, during the era 1870-1930, no less then 21 different narrow gauge railroads existed in Colorado at varying times. Some were short runs for tourists and minor freight work, while others were large enough in infrastructure to rival standard gauge lines in length and level of operation. As the mines played out, the narrow gauge lines barely struggled along, especially after highway development made the mountains truly accessible by other means.

However, the real so-called silver lining was that as the 1930s concluded, revenues picked up due to increased tourism into the still-remote areas of the state. Some lines got an additional reprieve when uranium, a radioactive ore that had formerly been carelessly discarded in mining operations, was found to have a most important military purpose during the Second World War.

Despite wholesale postwar abandonments and ever-greater

vehicle competition, certain segments remained profitable, particularly the Durango to Silverton line of the Rio Grande. Retired equipment was often donated to lineside towns as the rails were taken up, but the narrow gauge fever that stormed through Colorado boom towns 125 years ago still has its grip on thousands of fans and enthusiasts. Today, what now remains of the operating narrow gauge network continues to cross the wild heights of the Animas Canyon and Toltec Gorge in the southern part of the state as a tourist attraction in the warmer months.

The state of Maine has often been known to follow its own pathways, and they certainly did so when promoters decided that it would be even more economical to create rail systems on a 24" width. Using equipment that would have been more at home in many modern amusement parks, the Maine 'two-footers' were a source of interest for enthusiasts as soon as rail buffs found out they existed.

The largest of these operations was the Sandy River & Rangeley Lakes line, which ran from a connection with the Maine Central at Farmington into a variety of towns in the Longfellow Mountains. It was formed from a handful of predecessor companies in

Purposeful bridge construction highlights these early photo postcards of the East Tennessee & Western North Carolina, which edged its way along the gorge of the Doe River east of Hampton, Tennessee. Like many narrow gauge properties, this line's origins were in minerals, servicing ore banks located at Cranberry, N.C. Later, it was noted as a tourist attraction with its connection to and purchase of the Linville River Railroad, which eventually carried it into Boone, N.C. Today, little remains of the original operation into the Tarheel State, though the equipment became part of the popular Tweetsie Railroad in Blowing Rock. In the 1960s, five miles of trackage were re-laid in the Doe River Gorge for occasional tourist service, which still exists today. A handful of chrome postcards were also done of the recreational ride in the 1960s era, and a Christian camp owns the property today.

1909, primarily servicing Maine timber interests and Rangeley Lakes tourists. Many cards that show up are from this operation, which was 101 miles in length at its zenith. What remained of the SR&RL following the start of the Depression finally closed in 1935.

By that time, Maine's handful of other 24" lines (which, incidentally, were all isolated from each other) were also having hard times. Postcards from better days on the short Kennebec Central (between Gardiner and Togus, closed 1929), the Wiscasset, Waterville & Farmington (closed in 1934), the Bridgton & Harrison (closed in 1941), and the quarry-based Monson Railroad (closed in 1943) are all held in high regard by collectors. Real photo postcards of these narrow gauge rail operations in the Pine Tree State are among the most highly sought-after in the postcard hobby.

Like Colorado's little railroads, Maine's operations did not dis-

appear completely. What survived the 1930s scrapping operations ended up on a Massachusetts cranberry farm as the Edaville Railroad tourist line. In the 1990s, following that railroad's closing, most of the equipment was moved back to Maine and some of it has been returned to service at museums.

Many railroad enthusiasts pursue narrow gauge railroad memorabilia of any type. Colorado's mountain scenery and several regional postcard producers make certain examples from that state somewhat common. However, most locales will prove evasive. For collectors of narrow gauge lines elsewhere (they existed in many states during the first 20 years of the last century), expect the thrill of the hunt to be part of any pursuit. Frankly, a bit of luck will help as well. Note, however, that numerous chrome cards exist from the 1950s onward of narrow gauge equipment on display or in tourist service; a sizable collection built around these may help scratch the collecting itch between the needle-in-a-haystack finds of older examples.

*

The most visible feature of the railroad systems that linked North America together were the trains themselves. Yet, however romantic the notion of railroading was, the trains were but a small part of the picture. The successful operation of an even moderate railroad enterprise required a small army of support personnel and additional infrastructure beyond simply trains and tracks.

The Railroad Corridor

Considering the infrastructure of trackwork itself, the route's geography often made it impossible for the railroad to be built along simple and level straight lines. Moreover, creating ways to go from point A to point B had to be accomplished within the constraints of the line's operating equipment. Few gradients were steeper than three percent and curves followed the greatest possible radius available. To facilitate this, railroads had to cut through the lower ridges and fill gaps across shallow valleys with stone or rubble, while tunneling and bridging that track through the more difficult areas. This was all at no small expense. Areas where hard rock abounded could take months to blast through to make a suitably level track foundation or curve easement.

Once completed, however, the most dramatic locations along a railroad line would be those same bridges and tunnels, and these places were especially attractive to postcard producers. Early on, railroads used rock-based designs to complete some of the bridge structures. It is hard to fathom the manpower required to build a monolith like the Erie's Starucca Viaduct in northeastern Pennsylvania. While cast concrete was employed as well in some instances, by the turn of the century, steel structural shapes made from girders and beams were the most widely used medium for bridge building, supported by stone or con-

The lair of the steam engine. At right, a big J-class New York Central Hudson locomotive spins on the turntable at Elkhart, Indiana. The roundhouse was a simple but effective way to store the engines, since they normally needed to be turned to run in the opposite direction. Once out on the railroad, these locomotives made use of coaling docks like this one seen at left (likely on the Burlington) at Ferguson, Iowa.

Rear Admiral Young and Key West Mayor greeting Mr. H. M. Flagler on arrival of First Train to enter Key West, Fla. January 22nd, 1912.

(above) One of the most notable projects was the Florida East Coast's bridging of the Florida Keys by Henry Flagler, seen here arriving at Key West on the first train in 1912. Flagler's efforts were valiant, but the line failed after sustaining hurricane damage in 1935; the Key Highway now occupies much of its right-of-way.

(below) Bridges like Starucca Viaduct on the Erie Railroad, seen here with a Delaware & Hudson engine beneath, were built for the ages; it is still in use today. The now-defunct New York, Ontario & Western line chose all-steel construction for its bridge at Cadosia, Pa., where a helper engine appears to be backing downgrade after pushing a train over the summit.

Crater from Lovers Leap, Natural Tunnel

Tunneling took on many forms. Under the Hudson River, men worked in dark dampness to get the McAdoo subway system built during the early part of the century. This line is now part of the PATH system connecting New York and New Jersey.

crete uprights. These shapes could be transported over the completed rails to the locale and then erected by skilled men and heavy cranes.

Tunnels, on the other hand, were built by blasting train-sized bores through obstacles, and lining the hole with either wooden timbers or concrete. Tunnels had their own problems, particularly in terms of ventilating exhaust smoke from steam engines, which might also be fighting an uphill grade while passing though the bore. This was abated by exhaust fans on occasion, but lines with extremely long tunnels often ended up electrifying those segments.

Once the basic groundwork for a right-of-way was created, the rails would be laid down on heavy wooden crossties, under-girded by several inches of crushed rock to facilitate drainage away from the track. Where the

Sometimes the railroad made use of the terrain, as did the Southern (via predecessor Virginia & South Western) by passing through Natural Tunnel, a cavern carved by water in the mountains of Virginia that was large enough that a train could fit through it. Today, it is a state park, but trains of the Norfolk Southern continue to ply the rails there.

(clockwise from top left) Westinghouse Electric built many of the larger locomotives used in America's electrified rail territory; the engines seen on the shop floor date from 1910 or so. The rival coal-hauling Virginian and the Norfolk and Western lines each depicted their engines as the most powerful in the world. A new Great Northern electric motor leaves Cascade Tunnel soon after its completion. Generators in substations like the one in Piedmont, Montana, fed the wires for the Milwaukee Road's electrified division. Alas, none of this territory is still powered by electric engines today.

VIEW OF AISLE IN MAIN WORKS WHERE LARGE ELECTRIC LOCOMOTIVES ARE BUILT
WESTINGHOUSE ELECTRIC & MFG. CO.

THE MIGHTIEST LOCOMOTIVE IN THE WORLD
MANUFACTURED IN THE EAST PITTSBURGH WORKS OF
WESTINGHOUSE ELECTRIC & MANUFACTURING COMPANY, EAST PITTSBURGH, PA., U. S. A.

"ON THE CHICAGO, MILWAUKEE

INTERIOR OF SUB-STATION, PIEDMONT, MONT.

LARGEST ELECTRIC FREIGHT MOTOR IN WORLD. N. & W. RY. BLUEFIELD, W. VA.

trains traveled rapidly, curves might also be 'super-elevated,' with the outside curved rail somewhat higher than the inside rail. Sidings would be added so that trains could either pass other trains going the opposite direction, or overtake slower versions headed toward the same locale. Postcards of trackwork are somewhat commonplace, but rarely do scenes without trains generate any interest unless they show some other extenuating feature, such as people at work or lineside equipment like signals or buildings.

Signals and Maintenance

Where traffic became busy, signaling systems first developed during the Civil War became paramount to safe operation. Trains normally operate via track blocks, which is a predetermined length of track. In simple terms, a signal is red for 'stop' when the block immediately ahead is occupied by another train. It is yellow for 'proceed with caution' when the block fol-

lowing after the first is occupied, and it is green for 'go' when both blocks ahead are clear. These signals ranged from rope-tethered colored balls which could be raised or lowered, to semaphores with steel blades, to colored or position-type light supports.

Later, the larger railroads added automatic train control devices that would override the engineer who deliberately or inadvertently missed a signal's direction. On occasion, a railroad might issue a postcard announcing that signaling was in place for a safer trip. Normally, postcards feature signals only as peripheral to the trains themselves.

All of these systems required maintenance as well, and men were employed as track walkers, bridge maintainers, signal specialists, and more. The engineer got the glory, but it was this platoon behind him that made him look so good. One bad rail, and a fast runner in the locomotive's cab normally wasn't just hurt - he was dead. Like many jobs in heavy industry, pride in one's work was expected and required.

Steam locomotives were labor-intensive machines, and the term 'iron horse' was not a misnomer. They required a near-constant diet of treated water and select coal to operate properly. Facilities to 'feed' the engines were located strategically along the line. At the end of their run, they were cleaned of grime, and any remaining coal ashes were dumped from the firebox. The engine was then directed into its storage track position by a rotating platform called a turntable, and driven into a semi-circular building called a roundhouse for storage. Routine maintenance was done here and the engine would soon be back out on the open road again.

The Backshop

When needed, as per an inspection schedule or by necessity, the engine would be taken to a larger facility referred to as a backshop. Here, machines and men disassembled the engine and rebuilt whatever needed attention. Though extremely large, the steam locomotive was a precision machine, and the shop forces were skilled in the process of maintaining this efficiency. These buildings often featured huge drop-forges and wheel lathes, crewed by machinists and laborers. The advent of the diesel caused a large number of these jobs to disappear forever. Not all backshops were huge cavernous buildings - on smaller railroads, the engine house and backshop were sometimes one and the same, with rudimentary equipment and tools.

A second complex might have been designed to build or repair rolling stock, while yet another might be a stockpile of supplies to create or rebuild trackwork or buildings the railroad owned. Sometimes, these could all be found in one locale. On larger lines, they were spread out over the traffic divisions the railroad had designated. In the postcard era, engine and shop facilities (as well as the towns that had grown up nearby to serve them) were a fairly popular image, with locomotive servicing facilities at the top of the demand scale today.

The yards across the river bottoms at Kansas City show the basic layout of the engine terminal; the Rock Island's backshop, with its huge overhead crane, was large enough to handle the most demanding repairs. It was a brand-new structure when this card was issued circa. 1910.

Most of the largest railroad lines had been completed and were in operation by the start of the Twentieth Century. Documentation after 1900, when postcards were growing in popularity, would be mostly of upgrading previous construction.

However, a railroad promoter named George L. Carter saw the need for a new rail line that would connect the Midwest to the Southeast. Such a project had already been undertaken previously but had been financially unattainable. Carter and his associates bought what was available of these previous operations and formed a company they named the South & Western Railway in 1902. This line would cross the mountains below the coal fields of Clinch Mountain, passing through Virginia, Tennessee, and North Carolina before terminating in Spartanburg, South Carolina.

***BUILDING THE C.C. & O** (clockwise from top left)*
Narrow gauge "dinky"-type construction engines on the S&W; location and date unknown. The Climax locomotive at the top of the trestle was normally used for logging.

Sometime before 1915, one of the Clinchfield's big Mallet-type engines is headed north over the longest bridge on the line, the Copper Creek Viaduct in southwestern Virginia.

One of the best-known views was this one, showing three tunnels in a row on the climb from Spartanburg. It was reproduced through the era of the linen postcard.

A postcard showing a photographer's train that traversed the completed line in 1909, on the North Holston bridge .

Between Tennessee and North Carolina, the line follows the rugged Nolichucky Gorge, a remote locale.

To say the S&W faced a daunting task would be an understatement, as this terrain was rugged and filled with obstacles. Moreover, the railroad decided to build to the highest standards possible, meaning minor gradients and wide curve easements. In the end, the line began from about a 500 foot elevation, climbed to over 2500 feet above sea level, then dropped back down to sea level again. It featured over 17,000 feet of bridgework and 51,000 feet of tunneling, an amazing level of construction for less than 280 miles of trackage.

By 1908, the line had been reincorporated as the Carolina, Clinchfield & Ohio Railway. Trains were running the entire length from Dante, Va. to Spartanburg by 1909, though it would not be until 1915 that the

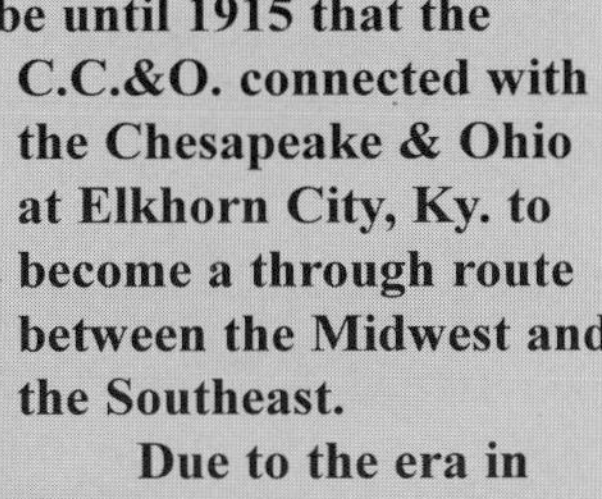

C.C.&O. connected with the Chesapeake & Ohio at Elkhorn City, Ky. to become a through route between the Midwest and the Southeast.

Due to the era in which it was built, during the postcard craze, a number of views exist of the effort to complete this project. One of the final mainline systems created in America, these rare real photo cards are an important part of the documentation of that effort.

Today, the Clinchfield line is part of the CSX system, and still maintains its role as a vital part of the nation's rail network.

Electricity For Power

While electric power had been adopted to power traction motors on trolley cars, by 1895 the Baltimore & Ohio's new underground electric motors could move whole trains through the Mt. Clare station area in Baltimore. This proved that this new power force could be harnessed elsewhere in railroading in addition to being mandated for smoke abatement purposes in larger cities. The Pennsylvania Railroad chose to electrify all of its major corridors between Washington and New York as well as west to Harrisburg, Pa., using electric power for both freight and passenger service as needed.

Ironically, west of Harrisburg ,where its grades were steepest, the Pennsy never went 'under the wire.' Further south in the Alleghany range, however, both the Norfolk and Western and Virginian lines chose this method for moving heavy coal out of the mountains. In the northwest, both the Chicago, Milwaukee, St. Paul & Pacific (the Milwaukee Road) and the Great Northern lines turned to this form of power due to long tunnels in the Rockies and difficulties in servicing steam engines in the mountain ranges. Several larger mining lines were also electric. Postcards showing these operations are quite popular among collectors of these lines.

The advent of the diesel spelled the demise of most of the electrification programs. Though the diesel was a candidate for rebuilding in the backshop on occasion, much of the steam-related infrastructure would be abandoned by the late 1950s. The water towers and coal elevators

The crew that made it all possible, somewhere, someplace, yesterday…

would no longer be needed, and they fell into various states of disrepair until the railroad company finally decided to tear them down. Since most diesel engines do not require mandatory turning like the steam locomotive did, the roundhouse has been largely replaced by tracks lined up side by side along a fuel rack. Only a few vestiges of the steam age remain in use or are still standing today.

Today's rail corridor itself has also undergone change when compared to the postcards of old. Where four tracks once ran, there are now two; where one track once ran, there is often none. For a regional or specific-railroad collector, vintage images offer clues to where buildings and track might have been - the footings of a water tower, the now-filled-in turntable pit, the cut blasted through solid rock. Like most armies, the vast battalion of railroad workers that won the nation's transport challenges back in the day is remembered now more for its monuments rather than its hard-fought victories.

*

Sanborn was a popular postcard producer throughout Colorado. This group of cards shows four versions of the narrow-gauge Rio Grande Southern's well-remembered "Galloping Goose" trains. These contraptions used an automobile body converted to 36" railroad use with a boxcar for mail and small freight service. There are a large number of rail enthusiasts who focus almost exclusively on the narrow gauge lines.

Union Pacific Challenger-type steam engines being serviced to the purpose-built "Galloping Goose" rail buses that ran on the narrow gauge Rio Grande Southern (seen on the page opposite). Like all railroads, the RGS and others in the state were hurt severely by the Great Depression. Only the need for now-desirable uranium from the tailings of ancient mine operations would keep some of these branch lines struggling along through the Second World War, then abandonment would start in earnest.

Into that scenario came enthusiast Bob Richardson, who started a tourist operation to save relics from the narrow gauge. This was called the Narrow Gauge Motel, and was located in the former railroad town of Alamosa. Richardson would issue several photo postcards showing final runs and train operations in the postwar era, with hand-lettered text as seen below. The motel became the basis of the world-class Colorado Railroad Museum located today in Golden. The postcards from both producers are in demand today as a lasting tribute to the Centennial State's truly immense railroad heritage. *

The mountain passes of Colorado have long held the high ground for many railroad enthusiasts. The fever for precious metals led financiers in the east and overseas to bankroll both standard and narrow gauge lines over the likes of Marshall Pass and into deep chasms as dark as the Black Canyon of the Gunnison River. Boomtowns and gold strikes fed the frenzy. After the silver rush petered away following the demise of the Sherman Silver Purchase Act in 1893, and the gold mines finally played out a decade or so later, these isolated railroads turned to tourism and local mail contracts as they slowly decayed during the Twentieth century.

However, railroad enthusiasts knew about the lines, and began to come into the 'shining San Juan Mountains' during the 1930s to ride and photograph these railroading antiquities. For real photo postcard collectors, two commercial outfits began offering images for sale at this time. One was Sanborn of Denver, who had produced postcards since the turn of the century, documenting Colorado and western life in general via black-and-white photo cards. Sanborn's shooters took pictures of everything, from the huge new

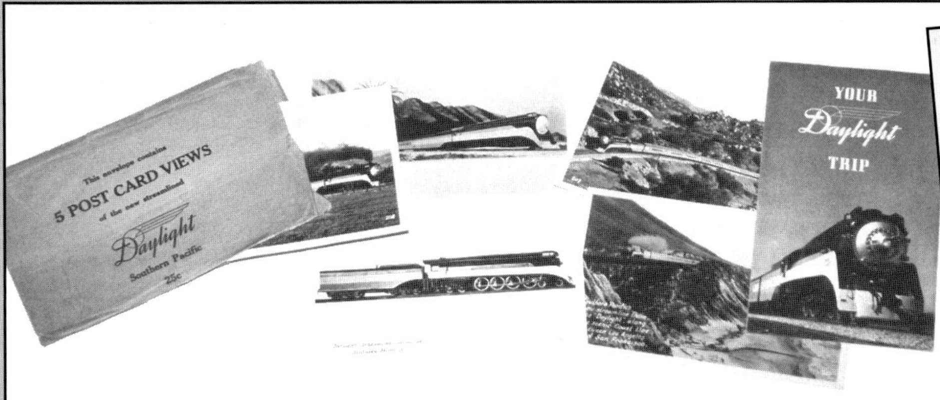

A set of cards issued in the 1930s by the Southern Pacific showing off the new streamlined Daylight trainsets. This example consists of five cards, an envelope, and a pamphlet on the trip itself. Most of these SP Daylight steam locomotive cards are quite common among railroad-issued real photo postcards.

A mong collectors of postcards, real photograph cards hold a special importance. Normal offset printing processes require literally thousands of cards to be produced to justify the expense of production; very few were done in quantities of less then 2500 examples. Real photo cards, on the other hand, are just what the name implies - real photographs. Often printed from the original negative on special black-and-white postcard paper by local or amateur photographers, in most cases, the production of these rarely exceeded 500 examples. In many cases, there was only a single copy produced from the negative.

Identifying real photo cards is fairly simple. In the 1900-1960 era, a variety of firms produced specific brands of paper for postcard use. Among these brands are AZO, Kodak Defender, Velox, EKC and others. This standard photographic paper, which features a gloss or near-gloss finish, usually has the maker's name imprinted where the stamp would be placed and the words 'post card' printed near the top. Several postcard books and internet sites offer specific information on identifying the paper by age and manufacturer.

Real photograph postcards such as the group opposite may depict similar equipment, but they all served different purposes. The upper right image shows a railroad-issued postcard done by the Canadian Pacific (near Yoho, British Columbia) in the 1920s, used to promote rail service in the Rockies. Note that a 'double-headed,' or multiple-engine consist was needed in the rugged territory. This series was continually recreated with different photos for several decades in the real photo format. The main center image is an example of a locally-produced card, in this case a Western Pacific steam train on the Tobin Bridges in northern California. Eastman Studios did many cards of varied subjects throughout this region; special care was obviously taken to get this particular picture with its soft sunlight and longer exposure. The bottom image is a railfan-issued photo card done by Richard Kindig showing one of the Rock Island Railroad's big R-class 4-8-4 Northern type engines thundering across the plains of eastern Colorado. These cards were often created specifically to trade with other railroad enthusiasts, not for retail resale.

C.P.R. Main Line Trans-Canada Limited near Field B.C.

TOBIN BRIDGES OVER THE FEATHER RIVER, CALIF.

Real-photo cards sometimes suffer the yellowing effects of poor initial photo development. Also, due to the somewhat stiff nature of the film emulsion on the paper, creasing of any kind can often lead to a crack, and, in severe cases, the destruction of a corner or edge. In other words, they can be fragile.

Real photo cards are not to be confused with black-and-white lithography, which uses a series of dots to create a continuous tone image. A real photo card will not show any patterning in the gray areas; it is a photograph. This is mentioned for two reasons. Primarily, there have been many black-and-white litho cards done over the years, some which may be misidentified as real photos. In addition to the patterning in the image, most can be identified by the use of offset type text on the front (i.e. a location's name) or an offset text caption on the back. Real photo cards which have any type of lettering normally have it written into the negative itself, often by hand, meaning it will appear in white on the picture. A few examples have a typed caption printed in a black area at the bottom.

The other reason for bringing up this issue is because some individual or firm actually reprinted vintage railroad postcards, complete with AZO stamp boxes on the back. These low-quality copies show the litho-dot patterning in the image area from the offset process, and are printed on soft medium-weight paper as opposed to the patternless, photo paper originals. These cards are not in any proliferation, and all knowledgeable

At top is a card showing a train yard crew and the small railroad switcher with they which they worked. Images showing labor have become increasingly popular among postcard collectors. This example probably dates to the 1910-1920s era. Below is a locally-produced early card, in demand because it shows a logging engine known as a Climax. These engines were purposely built for poor trackwork and are popular among railroad and timber industry collectors today. Another important asset to the card is the fact it is regionally identified. Handwritten into the negative below the engine, it states "Logging Team - Everett" (Wash. state).

dealers will answer questions about originality. However, using the increasingly popular online auction services will require the buyer to exersize some caution, especially when making expensive purchases. Don't be afraid to ask questions about cards being offered for sale. In some cases, the amatuer seller may not even be aware he or she is offering reproductions.

Real photo cards for the railroad enthusiast fall into three basic categories: railroad produced, commerciallyl/locally produced, and railfan produced.

Railroad Produced

The cost of doing a large quantity of real photo cards did not make this a practical way for railroads to create cards. In fact, with quality color lithography being popular and economical thoughout the postcard era, only rarely was this process used. There are some exceptions, however. The Canadian Pacific line offered several series of real-photo cards throughout the first half of the 20th Century.

The Canadian Pacific was a transcontinental line that spanned North America above the U.S. border. Its postcards served a primary role in introducing the rugged grandeur of the Canadian Rockies to potential riders. While each set consisted of various views, the CP often featured postcards showing trains in their sets, which are still plentiful.

As in most cases, cards that depict railroading are going to be more popular than those issued by the railroads but not depicting the railroad industry itself. The Canadian Pacific did their series in groups of 10 to 30 cards, and at least one group of these cards featured hand-tinted photographs. Today, most of the railroading scenes from these sets are still moderately priced, though some are quite scarce.

A few American railroads also created real photo postcards. As mentioned in the streamlining chapter, the most common of any real photo railroad cards are the trains-in-action series done by the Southern Pacific upon the introduction of their new streamlined *Daylight* steam trains in 1937. However, some of the dozen or so cards produced are more difficult to come by than others. At least two groups of SP action images were produced - one for the *Coast Daylight* which followed the Pacific Ocean for much of its run between Los Angeles and San Francisco, and the other for the *San Joaquin Daylight* that traveled through the fertile valleys more inland. The series is numbered between 200-210 in the image captions. Serious collectors should note

Equipment other than engines could be the focus of amateur or small-town photographers. In this scene, the one young man appears to be a little too close for comfort to this Great Northern snow plow during Windom, Minnesota's 1909 winter.

this railroad also did a much-harder-to-come-by series of cards on the interior of this Art Deco consist which would have to rank very high in terms of its scarcity, as well as a few other scarce cards featuring the new streamlined diesels. Another example would be the 1940s-era C& O issues (covered more indepth in the next chapter).

A final note on the railroad-issued real photos: unlike the normal real photo cards, these were sometimes done using a specifically produced paper due to the volume of cards produced (even if all the images were not the same). There might not be any paper identification such as a logo in the stamp box or other product mentions than simply the words 'post card' on the back. Offset text stating the producer's name (Gowen Sutton or Bryon Harmon) is present on the back of all the CP cards, while typeset rear captions and imprinted titles are on many of the C&O cards. The C&O and SP issues used DOPS and EKC papers.

Commercially and Locally-Produced Real Photo Postcards

Short-run commercial and locally-produced real photo cards were normally done by a photographer who could distribute his or her wares on a local, limited basis. These were cards printed for the purpose of resale, and railroad subjects proved to be among the most popular. Produced in numbers anywhere from one to 1,000, these cards are especially in demand among people collecting images from a certain region or locale, and can command some good prices as a result.

The primary commercial railroad subject was the depot image. As mentioned in the chapter on those cards, this was a community meeting place in the days before mass-produced automobiles, television and air travel. The local photographer might take a picture of the station with a few people present or with a crowd. In some cases (although by no means as often as one would think), the image would be captured with a train actually in the station. A few were even photographed with trains speeding past, quite a trick considering the level of photographic equipment and films available at the time.

The next major type of locally-produced real photo postcard would be the disaster image. During the early part of the century, as traffic management, track work and signaling systems were being refined, incidents ranged from mild derailments to fatal head-on collisions. These occurred with uncomfortable regularity. If such happenings were close to where the photographer could arrive before the cleanup was finished, *viola!* instant success. There are numerous rail disaster cards available, and pricing varies based on quality and demand. Unlike air disasters such as the Hindenburg explosion, or sea disasters like the Titanic, there have been very few rail

A smoky eastbound B&O coal train roars past the able camera of newpaper man William Price of Cumberland, Md., who recorded it as a 6000-series 2-10-2 at Patterson Creek Tower. The date - June 26, 1947. It was the efforts of men like Price who recorded the final passing of the steam era; his irreplaceable negatives are in safe hands today, in a historical society collection.

incidents that have garnered a level of true infamy in the minds of the general American populace, so no one card or accident has proven popular above the others. Cards showing clear signs of boiler explosions and locomotive damage will normally be more highly desired than those simply depicting train equipment flipped off the tracks. Postcards showing actual fatalities are not common and will command a premium, although not necessarily from the rail enthusiast market. See the section on wrecks and disasters for more details.

Finally, railroads often appear as secondary parts of street scenes and industrial images done by the commercial or local producer. This might show a railroad track or cars at a local industry, a railroad right-of-way or structure in the area, or railroad infrastructure in a birds-eye style aerial view. These cards will appeal to the same audience as the depot cards: locality-specific collectors and rail enthusiasts.

Sometimes, an amateur photographer would have the negatives he or she exposed printed on postcard paper. These unlabeled and unidentified images are often single copies. Contingent on the scene's quality, the railroad, and a location's popularity, all such real photo postcards are important and treasured pieces in many collections. Due to the fact that they were not overly dramatic (though a disaster photo might have been), images of this type were probably more likely to be discarded in the ensuing years. While some of this scarcity is tempered by the narrow market demand for a particular view, most collectors will purchase these real photos if the card at all interests them, since they realize the opportunity may never present itself again. Finally, knowing the history of a railroad can help identify unlabeled cards.

William P. Price
402 Fayette St.
Cumberland, Md.

POST CARD

10192

DuPont Defender

CORRESPONDENCE

ADDRESS

B&O eastbound coal drag headed by 6000 series 2-10-2 at first signal bridge east of Patterson Creek Tower on 3 track section of Cumberland Division. Center lane signaled in both directions.

4/26/47

A classic action shot done by Denver's Otto Perry. Perry traveled extensively when vacationing and is well-known among the rail enthusiast community. His work is still considered among the best of all railroad photographers. The handwritten information by the artist found on the backs of many railfan cards adds to their intrinsic if not financial value.

Railfan Produced Postcards

Railfan postcards are a very unique segment of the real photo market, one which some postcard enthusiasts have never understood fully. The group of serious railroad enthusiasts that developed in the 1920-1940 era found that a ready way to savor the details of their hobby was to record it on film. Moreover, a simple and cheap way to exchange photos with like-minded individuals was to print the picture on a piece of postcard photo paper.

These cards were rarely produced with the intention of being sent through the mail. Indeed, some of the photographers saw fit to develop a large customized rubber stamp that would allow them to date and document the photo card they created. Stamped on the back, this info would cover both the letter and address area on the card. Then, through correspondence or acquaintance, they would trade these cards back and forth, or sell them through the mail. It allowed someone in, say, Ohio to get images of locomotives from Maine without having to travel. There were a fair number of these cards created.

The first serious hardbound pictorial railroad book was printed in 1938. Prior to the release of that book, **High Iron,** by noted journalist Lucius Beebe, postcards were one of the few ways to see quality pictures from other parts of the country. Several regional photographers contributed to Beebe's efforts. **Trains** magazine, the first photo-oriented periodical for the railroad enthusiast, came into being just before the Second World War. These same photographers now had a place to sell their pictures, both commercially as postcard prints to the public as well as for editorial use in the magazine. As a result of their subsequent exposure to the public, some of them became very well-known within the railfan commmunity.

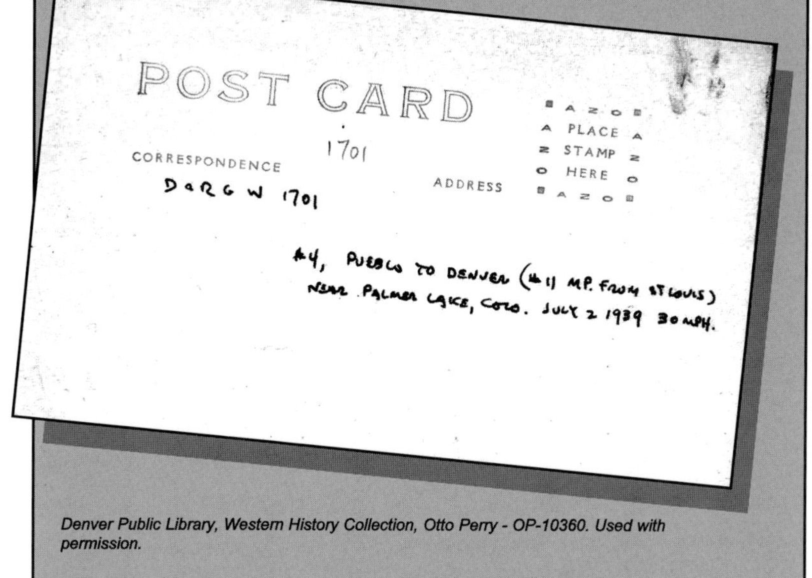

Denver Public Library, Western History Collection, Otto Perry - OP-10360. Used with permission.

POST CARD

RAILROAD PHOTOGRAPHS
47 ROYAL STREET
ALLSTON, MASS. ADDRESS

PLACE A STAMP HERE

CORRESPONDENCE

CHICAGO & NORTH WESTERN

CHARGE #120

An example of a card by **Railroad Photographs,** *showing a very busy rush hour mix of Chicago & North Western steam trains. Visible in this image are four different trains moving commuters in and out of the Windy City sometime in the early 1930s. Though Railroad Photographs created an extensive file of images during this era, the negatives it amassed have not been publicly accounted for as of this date.*

These railfan images can be broken down into two groups: roster and action. Roster shots are fairly common in many postcard dealers' stock. These are images of a locomotive standing still or in a setting by itself. The more prolific photographers got to know the railroad employees personally and could sometimes get an engine positioned to make the optimum use of the sun's light and the locomotive's mechanical beauty. However, in many cases, these would simply be an image of the engine taken where it was standing.

There are three major factors that play into the demand for roster photos: the quality of the image, the engine itself, and the railroad depicted. Since many enthusiasts have a greater interest in one railroad over another, they will buy based on their favorites. On the other hand, engines featuring streamlining or classic styling, and most narrow gauge equipment, will be in demand no matter what. All thing being equal, passenger engines tend to be more popular then freight units. One final factor which can influence a card's appeal is the railroad infrastructure visible in the image: a water column or coaling tower sometimes adds to the sense of the card's importance.

The best known of the 'roster' men was Robert Foster, whose efforts were highlighted in a chapter in Joe Collias' hardbound tribute **The Search for Steam** in the early 1970s. There were many, many others, however, who could make a standing locomotive into a piece of artwork; their efforts are well worth pursuing.

While virtually anyone with a steady hand and tripod could take a roster shot, action photos required a bit more skill. A fast lens was paramount if the result was to be a sharp image, and most of the really good action photographers used Speed or Crown Graphics, high-end press photographer cameras. These men would often scout out locations beforehand, and then set up and wait for the train to come through. The criteria for judging a card's worth is the same as with the roster shot, but in this author's opinion, the action image should be more popular as it shows the railroad working, just as a quality baseball or sporting image showing an individual athlete in play is more impressive than a simple portrait. Of course, the sharpness of the final

Though St. Louis roster photographer Robert Foster knew this was only a small freight 2-8-0 Consoilidation-type steam engine on the Missouri Pacific, his use of great lighting, a small f-stop, and an adjacent coaling tower make this image a classic. The work of some of the railfan-oriented photographers rivals the photographic art being produced by the best professionals of that era.

product (the skill of the photographer might be a better description) will play greatly into the demand.

Among the action postcard producers were several men still held in high regard by railfans. Richard Kindig and Otto Perry were both from Colorado and both shot extensive groups of high quality action images - Perry's 20,000+ negatives are now archived in the Denver Public Library collection. Newspaperman William Price of Cumberland, Md., also did postcards of trains in his area, documenting the Western Maryland and Baltimore & Ohio lines.

The primary early commercial action supplier was a firm called Railroad Photographs, run by locomotive engineer H. Pontin from his home in Massachusetts. This company did many postcards by several different photographers, some of which were actually used in publication. Pontin supplied some images to Beebe for the aforementioned **High Iron** tome and other books. All four mentioned above also did roster views on occasion, though Perry likely had the best eye for the dramatic when an engine was standing still.

The railfan-produced postcard images faded as the steam engines dropped their fire. Many of these photographers had no heart for recording the less dramatic diesel "invaders." Plus, the advent of higher-speed Kodachrome films and 35mm cameras was changing the face of photography by the beginning of the 1960s, when the steam era finally ended. Black-and-white photo postcard printing and trading disappeared for the most part at this time as well.

Ironically, for many rail collectors, real photo postcards are an acquired taste. There is a fear on the part of some people that these items could be easily reproduced using still-existent negative collections. While reprints may be available on regular photographic paper, they do not have the period feel of the vintage postcard paper, nor the intrinsic value of having been created and identified by the original artist. Many collectors soon discover that they appreciate these scarce images more then most other cards in their collections. Currently, there is little price difference between the well-known photographers and other real photo railroad images.

∗

Railroads were always big business. Therefore, as postcards moved into the foremost realms of promotion, advertising departments went to work creating the best possible graphics and visual impact. From the earliest days of the postcard craze, the cards the railroads issued themselves would often outshine images coming from the public sector. When photography was the chosen medium, even in retouched form, the rail industry hired the best professionals, men who could translate corporate ideals onto film.

Of course, the railroad's corporate photography (and artwork) was used for many other purposes beyond postcards. Annual reports, publicity and press releases, and company brochures were among the different items also filled with these images. However, for the postcard enthusiast, the realm of corporate photography opens up an immense and interesting niche in collecting.

As one might surmise, prior to the advent of the chrome-type postcards of the 1940s, most of the unaltered corporate photography were black and white releases. The Canadian Pacific and Southern Pacific (unrelated other than in name similarity) were the biggest producers of these, though they were not the only ones. Other

Some western lines offered black-and-white real photo postcards in the late 1930s. At top is an image of the crack Southern Pacific / Union Pacific / Chicago & North Western City of San Francisco streamliner from 1937, while below is the interior of the UP's new Challenger from the same era. Both of these cards are fairly scarce today. Most of the railroad issued corporate photography postcards feature excellent exposures and well-designed views. By noting the car seen through the window at the far left, the Challenger photo was in all likelihood taken at a static location using models for the passengers.

This is a Ford Motor Company industrial shot of the docking facilities at the Rouge River plant from the 1920s. It is quite interesting in that it shows both steam and electric rail power, ships, trucks, and even a Ford Tri-Motor airplane flying overhead. This is from a series of cards Ford did of the immense Rouge River works near Detroit.

prior to that time. The true era of the corporate photograph on railroad postcards began in the 1930s. Photos done for publicity purposes would often feature matched train consists (all the cars exactly the same) running behind the very latest in motive power. In the streamlined era, this fresh appearance was of paramount importance when promoting passenger service.

companies, such as the Santa Fe and the Frisco (SF-SL), would make use of retouched images reprinted in color by the Detroit Publishing Company. Still others, like the Burlington, preferred the lithographic black-and-white process. A series of photo-realistic black-and-white litho cards was released by the Great Northern in the late 1920s.

Until the advent of the Depression, commercial illustrators did a majority of the artwork found on cards by the bigger railroads. Few corporate photographs were released by these railroads on postcards

However, the pursuit of corporate photography becomes even more interesting in the post-World War II era. Using Kodachrome film, the railroads began to record scenes in glorious color. Some railroads, notably the Union Pacific and the Southern Pacific, did a great deal of postcard reproduction based around color photography until the end of their respective passenger "glory days." The New York Central, who had reproduced yearly calendar artwork on most of its postcards before the war, hired men like Ed Nowak and O. Winston Link to photograph

William Rittase's Corporate Masterpieces

As the Second World War progressed in the mid-1940s, it became obvious that new engines were needed to move critical materials from the nation's heartland to the places where they were needed for the war effort. The products of the rich coal seams of West Virginia and Kentucky required rail movement across mountain ranges and valleys, so the Chesapeake & Ohio Railroad turned to the Lima Locomotive Works to create what was, in the minds of many, the most powerful steam locomotive ever produced. Using their 'Super Power' technology, Lima turned out a 2-6-6-6 wheel arrangement that met the needs of the railroad and then some.

Named the Alleghany in deference to the mountains it was built to tame, this locomotive became a primary subject of a scarce and highly desirable group of black and white real photo postcards the rail-

its trains, and a few were released as postcards.

Not all of this material was railroading itself; some corporate photography views were of the scenic points reached by the railroad. The Union Pacific did this often. These cards, however, do not hold nearly the interest to most enthusiasts as the railroad views do.

As the railfan hobby hit its stride in the 1960s, aftermarket postcard companies began to print cards not to promote current rail-

roading but to recall better times. Audio-Visual Designs (A-VD), the late Carl Sturner's company out of New York, and Lyman Cox of Sacramento, were two of the most prolific producers. Through their efforts in working with the railroad companies, dozens upon dozens of corporate images from former times found their way onto postcards in the 1960s and 1970s. Many of these photos had not been used before, even by the railroad companies. While later years would see some of

road issued in the mid-to-late 1940's. Taken by noted industrial photographer William M. Rittase of Philadelphia during the 1944-1948 period, they are extremely well-thought-out and executed. Recognized as one of the nation's premier professionals, Rittase did not disappoint his employers back then nor those who appreciate seeing his efforts today.

Traveling the system, Rittase documented primarily freight railroading; there are a handful of single passenger car images as well. Hump yards, switch towers, mines and the gorges of West Virginia appear on the cards, as well as some West Virginia city views. One card even has an image of the C&O's experimental #500 "Chessie" steam turbine of the late 1940s, complete with a dynamometer car behind it.

At this point, it is not known how many Rittase images exist on postcards; perhaps a dozen or so. Distribution of the cards is also still a question. What can be stated is that they are among the most difficult railroad issued cards to find in the hobby today, and those examples that show up rarely stay in a dealer's stock for any amount of time....

these images collected in book form, for the most part, the postcards were the easiest way to collect color pictures at that time.

Cox actually took his reproduction of these pictures into a 6" x 9" format that he marketed as his Vanishing Vistas series. These cards made use of images from many sources, but were noted for the high quality of printing on postcard stock. Since no room was left for an address or stamp after the first year or so of production, some may argue they are not true postcards, but they are certainly collectible and few railroad postcard collectors can resist them.

Today, there are still some occasions for corporate railroad photography. Amtrak, of course, still produces postcards for their patrons, but in this era of super-mergers, cards from the individual railroads have become something of a thing of the past. The larger continental size used for most current postcard production would likely

NORTH AMERICAN COLD STORAGE
2171
ILLINOIS CENTRAL
202
2
2

The Company's Finest *(clockwise from top left) A photographer uses a large format camera to take a builder's photo of the latest Norfolk & Western A-class steam engine. Among the corporate images offered to collectors by Audio-Visual Designs was this Chicago & North Western file photo of two streamliners in front of Chicago's Merchandise Mart. The Southern Pacific trains inside and out; the center image was never offered as a postcard before Lyman Cox printed it. Railroads like the Illinois Central were proud to feature both their fast diesel streamliners and their respected steam locomotives when creating postcards in the early postwar era. This particular card was printed by the railroad itself, but the image has been reissued by the railfan aftermarket as well.*

be the format.

From a collectibility standpoint, the chrome cards done by the aftermarket have actually shown more value pricewise than some of the railroad issues. However, it must be noted that the hobby still judges chromes as "chromes," period, making little differentiation between the older and newer cards.

Therefore, this is one area where the economically-minded yet diligent collector can still make real finds. Color sets, complete with envelope, issued by both the Southern Pacific and the Santa Fe, can still be found fairly easily. The earliest chromes by Cox and A-VD with previously unpublished classic corporate photos are likely in the highest demand today. Mary Jane's Railroad Specialties used corporate images on occasion, and Bob Fremming also reproduced some corporate photos in black-and-white. See the chapter on modern cards (p. 104-107) for additional information on chrome postcards.

*

The growing successes of the nation's rail operations led to a near-continual evolution in technology and performance. As the trains began picking up speed and running with greater frequency, inadequacies would reveal themselves, many times at the expense of life and limb. Railroading was a dangerous business (and still holds its share of risks today).

The infrastructure itself was sometimes the culprit, as poor track work and primitive signaling failed. Likewise, severe weather could destroy bridges or wash out the supporting earth and gravel beneath the rails. If a train was moving at a slow pace, disaster could normally be avoided; the same was rarely true with the bigger, faster equipment that had become standard at the dawn of the twentieth century and the postcard age.

In this pictorial section, we will examine and identify a few examples of the wreck postcard genre. The collecting of accident and wreck postcards is a popular one. This is an area dominated by real photo images. There were a few others done as litho images, but most are the 'real deal.' Prices for cards of this nature can vary based on the quality of the image, its rarity or infamy, condition, and factors such as mentioned or visible mortality. A critical factor is the level of identification provided either as text in the picture or as handwritten notes on the rear; there are far more unidentified wrecks then those with information. It is therefore best not to overspend for unidentified images unless they are particularly dramatic.

A final note - on many occasions, a photographer would record multiple views of an accident. It is always best to own the entire sequence so that details and information can be gleaned from them if needed. While some may consider collecting these cards a macabre pursuit, they are certainly part of the fabric that makes up the history of American railroading.

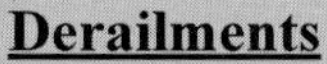

Derailments
When the tons of steel that made up a steam engine came off the tracks, serious damage was the end result. Seen above is a Southern Pacific cab forward engine (so named because of its unique design) tying up both the railroad and telegraph traffic. Below left, a Central Vermont locomotive is 'on the ground' due to an open switch (note the wooden tie cribbing in the foreground that will be used to help upright the engine). On the 1909 litho postcard at center left, a Milwaukee Road crew is getting a work train boxcar back on the rails.

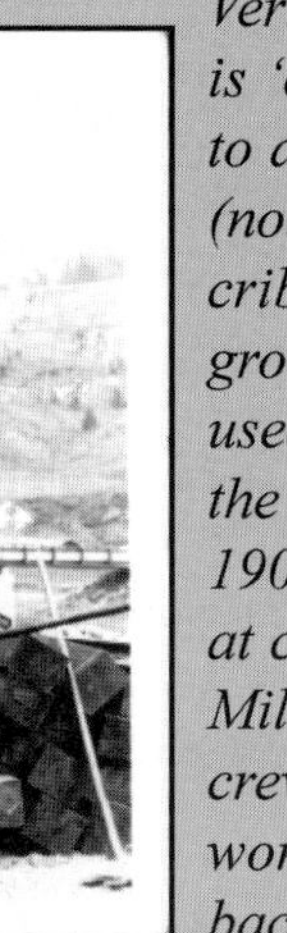

Boiler explosions

A Colorado rail photographer named J.D. Riley had the grim misfortune of taking photographs of Denver & Rio Grande Western articulated engine 3703 on October 19, 1952. Less than an hour later, the boiler exploded. This was normally caused by a lack of water, which exposed the boiler's steel crown sheet to the furnace of coals underneath, subsequently allowing that pressure to burst. Dick Kindig, who printed the entire group, was called to photograph the clean-up at Louviers,Colo., where the boiler was thrown completely over and the lead truck of the engine eerily coasted a quarter-mile down the tracks by the momentum. The large shrapnel often produced by a boiler explosion like this was easily capable of leveling an entire house.

Head-on collision

Few incidents were as dramatic as a pair of opposing trains having the misfortune of being on the same track at the same time. The impact would normally be fatal to one or both crews, and this problem would be exacerbated by fast night running and low signal visibility. As a direct result, railroads developed an extensive number of forms and permissions that train crews picked up as they sped past wayside stations, telling which crew had the right of way. That didn't prevent Virginian's steam-led passenger train #3 from mating with an electric-powered eastbound coal train on a blind curve in 1928 (left), nor this pair of Clinchfield engines from mixing it up sometime during the same era (far left). Today, this type of problem is largely avoided by the use of in-cab signaling and automatic train controls.

Snowbound

Though very possible early in the century, being stuck in snow drifts was a rarity by 1952. That year, the Southern Pacific's crack westbound **City of San Francisco** *had the misfortune of becoming mired in snow slides on the slopes of Donner Pass. The images seen here were likely shot by one of the passengers, who was among the 226 stranded at the infamous location for three days as the railroad worked frantically to rescue them. The images are deceiving, as the stalled train was poised atop a high mountain ledge of the Sierra Nevada range.*

Freight Fires and Explosions

The railroad served a vital and pressing need in shipping the nation's industrial goods, normally without problems. This card from sometime early in the last century graphically shows the results of a head-on collision in Pennsylvania (either the PRR or Reading Railroad). The impact has lifted the tender off the rails and a chemical fire has begun in the cars just behind. Oft-times, brave workers would try to uncouple the undamaged cars so another engine could pull them clear from behind. The man climbing the pole is likely attempting to get to the telephone lines and relay a message from the crew working on the fire. Today, such incidents are rare, but can still result in large numbers of people being evacuated away from the accident area.

Washouts & Collapsing Bridges

Sudden violent storms and rising water levels could cause track work and small bridges to be destroyed. In the two Santa Fe incidents shown here, bridge work has wreaked havoc on operations. In the 1930s view at right, the piled passenger cars in the New Mexico desert have lost some of their contents, including, in this case, a baggage car casket shipment. Note that the wheelsets are gone (these were not permanently attached to the cars). The other images below show a self-powered McKeen passenger unit and trailer that have gone off of a bridge at Randolph, Kansas sometime before 1920. The washout area is under where the car has come to rest, which is on the wrong side of the bridge abutment. This pair is part of a photo sequence in which the photographer noted '15-20 minutes after the wreck' on some of the cards (not shown).*

Name Passenger Trains

While accidents could happen anywhere, the most prominent location was along a lightly-traveled branch line. When a famous train or rail corridor was involved, like the derailed 20th Century Limited seen here at St. Johnsville, NY, postcards would likely be issued. Unfortunately, this example is un-dated. A more devastating occurrence found two Pennsylvania Railroad steel cars impacting one another at Mt. Union, Penn., on Feb. 27, 1917. This is called telescoping, where one car is so severely impacted that it actually rises enough to slide through another. Tragically but typical for this type of accident, all 20 people in the lower sleeping car Bellwood *were killed in this incident.*

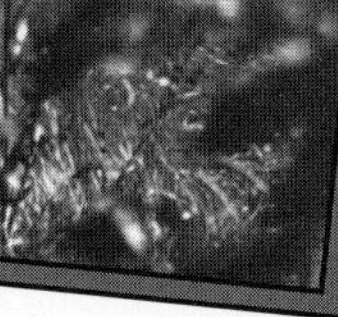

T oday, the use of electricity is so commonplace that it is very hard to image a time without it. As electric power emerged across the nation towards the end of the 19th century, street lights and other practical applications were accompanied by a new mode of transportation that was based around vehicles using electric traction motors that rode on rails.

The Birth of the Street Car

Traction motors convert electric current through a generator which in turn causes wheels to spin. In 1888, a gentleman named Sprague from Richmond, Va. was the first to use such power with

The interurban was nationwide. Above left is a car of the Wabash Valley line in the streets of Warsaw, Indiana, while above right shows a high speed car of the Lake Shore Electric crossing the New York Central's main line near Sandusky, Ohio. At right, the full-fledged depot and big cars on the Oregon Electric line at Harrisonburg, Ore., proves that this was not a fly-by-night operation, but real railroading under the wire; this line offered both freight and passenger service.

Trolleys and street cars were part of everyday life during the early years of the last century, and were considered a vast improvement in travel over the many horse-and-buggy consists present in this Pontiac, Mich., view.

universally welcomed in most locales. Unlike the steam power of the railroads, the street car emitted no smoke and traveled virtually in silence except for the warning bell to keep pedestrians clear of the car. This bell was soon supplemented by catch-net devices in the event someone failed to get out of the way in time.

Next Stop: Trolley Cars

The urban effort was quickly followed up by lines that linked smaller towns with larger cities, and lines that gave riders a chance to visit the country for a day. These became best known as trolley cars, and were found in all sorts of configurations from open-platform party cars to

success in a rail-car, which had formerly been drawn through the streets by a horse. Today's diesels continue to use traction motors (powered by internal combustion engines), but in those days, the logical way to power the generators was from an overhead wire. By the turn of the century, hundreds of miles of wire and rail had been laid for this purpose, and with good reason.

Urban street cars, especially in large cities which had formerly been full of defecating horses, were the first big application of the technology; this change was almost

This unidentified real photo card shows a typical car barn in areas where winter weather could hurt wooden cars. It is likely someplace in Ohio. The shop forces included linesmen, who were responsible for the maintenence of the overhead power source; these look like track maintenance crews.

hearses. The trolley network was so complex that a book was written in 1904 by a honey-mooning couple who had ridden from Delaware to Maine on the various lines. The big benefit over the steam railroads was that trolleys ran on the hour or quicker, while the trains might only arrive once or twice a day. The trolley fare was also quite economical in comparison. At their zenith in 1915, over 15,000 route miles of electrified traction lines existed, though they would fade from the scene very quickly as the personal automobile became prevalent.

The Need For Speed: Interurban Cars

The trolley trip was noted as leisurely by most accounts, though the traction motors could whip a car up to 40 mph or quicker with little effort. This didn't often happen where the line wound through bucolic countryside meanderings, but when a company laid rail to steam road standards, rapid service became a hallmark. These lines became known as interurbans, and they often connected two large locales, say between Cleveland and Columbus, Ohio. Though the fastest steam trains still held sway in terms of speed numbers, these lines could run cars at or above the 'mile-per-minute' margin (60-mph).

The interurban lines were closer to the real railroads than their trolley and street car brethren. They often featured sturdier initial or upgraded construction, good equipment, and modern railroad safety practices. In some areas, they took the place of a steam railroad and gave a community a chance to connect with the rest of the nation.

More often, particularly in the highly-developed industrial heartland of the Midwest, they were competing for business and running times comparable to many steam rail lines. Unlike street cars or trolleys, interurbans would often run multiple-car trains, and in some cases, offered freight car services like the railroads.

As Roger Grant notes in his book **Ohio's Railway Age in Postcards,** few self-respecting towns were without a street railroad by 1910. Those without such conveyances sometimes benefited from postcard producers who "installed" one that was non-existent except on a printed card. In most instances, however, the rails really were laid into

the unpaved dirt, or on brick or cobbled streets.

Collecting Traction Postcards

Like the narrow gauge rail routes, trolley and interurban lines have their own group of specialized collectors, sometimes referred to as 'traction fans.' As the electric rail companies were a part of everyday life through the post-card craze of 1907-1915, they appear on tens of thousands of different cards. Other similar forms of transportation would include subways and elevated lines from large cities, cable-operated cars like those that San Francisco installed, and inclined planes whose purpose was to move people from one elevation to another. In Cincinnati, a city noted for trolley service, there were inclined planes that actually transferred entire trolley cars up and down from the city heights.

In terms of demand, the real photo cards that were shot by local firms are at the pinnacle. Since this form of transportation has long since disappeared from the scene, these cards are often the only reference a locale-specific collector may have to a former operation. Few portrait-type photographers would have seen fit to put a trolley on

A self-propelled McKeen wind-splitter on the Central New York & Southern steam line.

film except on special occasions. In some cases, cards were created to show the opening of a new line or extension, but more often the frequently-seen trolleys were a part of the momentary scene. When trolleys are seen passing through a specific town with identifiable store-fronts and buildings, these cards often hold additional interest.

By far the most common cards would be those showing any number of street cars in the larger cities. Many cards were also done of the trolley in medium-sized locales or even out on the open road. These were normally done by local publishers.

The trolley firms themselves tended to be progressive enterprises, and on some occasions would issue their own postcards. One such set, shown on these two pages, was a sequence of eight total. This depicts a Stroudsburg & Delaware Water Gap Scenic Railway's trolley climbing a curve-filled hillside, including a view of the scenery as seen from inside the car (above, opposite). Some cards done by the companies would simply promote the trolley service itself, while others, particularly towards the end of the era, promoted new equipment.

Trolley Parks, Infrastructure, and Accidents

One interesting aspect of the trolley line was the development of recreation parks at the end of a route. Since the company was already generating its own power in many cases (and actually would sell it to consumers along the right-of-way on occasion), operating a group of amusements was one way to get people to ride the cars. These parks were promoted as healthy for the soul weary of city life as well as an entertainment to the family. Postcards of these parks themselves are collectable. A few of these parks survive to this day, though the trolleys are long gone.

The infrastructure of the interurbans and the trolley lines is also found on postcards, identified by the overhead line or caption. Powerhouses, depots, right-of-way bridging and tunneling, and other related images range in scarcity levels. At night, the cars often ended up under covered sheds or in buildings; these car barns are also found on an occasional postcard.

The early cars were made out of wood, and this led to no small amount of destruction if they were hit by a train or another electric car. In the midwest, several real-photo postcards were made of a particularly devastating telescoping accident on the Wabash Valley line in 1910 that took 41 lives. Other cards exist that show cars having derailed in the street, caught on fire, hit by trains at crossovers, and other types and degrees of mayhem. These may be found in a dealer's disaster category as well as in the trolley section. The faster interurbans would turn to steel construction as that method of car building became more predominant.

One final note might be to state that the railroads did not take this lying down. In some cases, they bought the competing trolley lines; J. P. Morgan and Charles Mellon's purchase of the New England region's vast array of traction roads for the purpose of monopoly is well-documented. However, some railroads saw this new technology as a good thing and began buying singular or car-

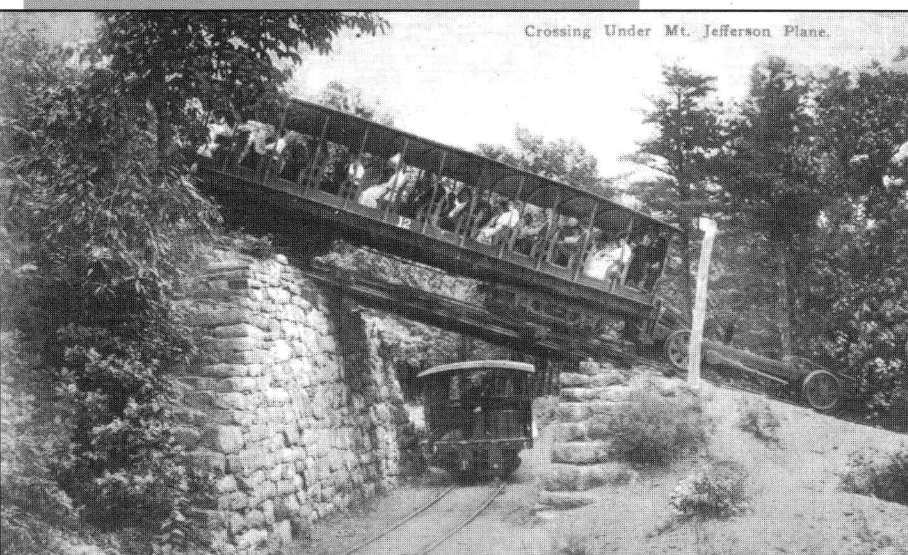

Two cards showing inclines - one is the fabled Jefferson plane in Jim Thorpe (formerly Mauch Chunk), Pa., while the other was one in Cincinnati capable of moving an entire car.

and-trailer oil burning railcars to supplement their more expensive
steam services. The most popular were built by McKeen of Omaha
and are known as 'wind-splitters' due to their pointed vertical noses.
These cars also featured round port-hole style windows, and are
attractive to many card collectors. These were later superceded by
other gas-electric units and self-propelled rail cars known as RDCs,
which the Budd Company built.

The age of the trolley ended in some ignominy. Short-sighted
urban planners of the era wanted the cars out of the streets, and the
auto manufacturers, seeing the ingrained competition, worked
behind the scenes to help that effort along. In some locations, the municipalities took over the bankrupt or failing
enterprises in the interest of the community. More often,
the result was rails being sent to the scrapyards and stacks
of old trolleys set afire as the easiest form of destruction.
None of the large interurban systems have survived as
they were initially conceived or incorporated.

Perhaps the most significant system was that of the
Pacific Electric on the West Coast, which linked most of
southern California together in a 1000-mile network of
trackage. In the interest of 'modernization,' the electric
line was systematically displaced by buses until it failed.
By the 1960s, nothing was left of what had been perhaps
the most logical system in the country. Ironically, similar
urban planners are spending billions in that region today
to replace just a little of what once existed.   *

Postwar Illinios Terminal Streamliner

*T*he interurban craze was not isolated to any one specific region. Companies operated in Maine and Washington State, from sea to shining sea. However, where these cars had their greatest impact was likely in Illinois, with the hub being Chicago.

Several large traction firms linked points throughout the Midwest to the Windy City. By the 1920s, these had all been brought under an umbrella holding company by Samual Insull, who was in charge of Commonwealth Edison and led a concern called the Middle West Utilities Corporation. Having started with the famed Chicago "L" loop, this effort soon included the Chicago, South Shore &

New cars for
the South
Shore - 1950s

THE ILLINOIS TRACTION SYSTEM OPERATES FIVE HUNDRED MILES OF ELECTRIC RAILWAY. CONNECTS ST. LOUIS, MO.

The Electroliner-
The North Shore's streamlined hope

Depression would ruin the holding company's valiant effort, as well as the overextended utility business, and Sam Insull's reputation.

On its own again, the Chicago, Aurora & Elgin (C.A.& E.) would die slowly through the 1950s. The North Shore was infused with its new streamlined Electroliners that arrived in 1941. These trains that could top easily 80 mph on the CNS&M's well-ballasted corridor, and helped the line struggle on into the postwar era. However, like so many predecessors, it's value in scrap was worth more than any potential income. Its history ended in the opening days of 1963. The South Shore (CSS&SB) is the sole survivor from the interurban era, and it continues to soldier down most of its original route as a public-run utility.

No book on railroad postcards would be complete without mention of the Illinois Traction System, which was formed from several smaller companies in 1909 and ran between Peoria, Ill. and St. Louis, Mo.. This interurban produced several outstanding and scarce advertising postcards (one is seen at lower left, opposite). Like the North Shore, the ITS took on streamlining to help boost revenues. Alas, that didn't work, and the postwar years found passenger service abandoned, though it would continue on into the 1980s as a diesel-motived carrier named the Illinois Terminal.

Needless to say, cards from all these lines are hard to come by today, and are actively sought after by postcard collectors. Like the diesel streamliners, the traction streamliners were part of the final act of a vanishing, long-distance passenger era.   *****

South Bend line that ran from South Bend, Indiana eastward; the Chicago, North Shore & Milwaukee, which offered high speed service from the north; and the Chicago, Aurora & Elgin line, which came in from the western suburbs.

This effort had several good benefits. It created physical power corridors for the huge generating plants Insull had built, meaning ready electricity could be brought to the growing suburbs. It gave the varied lines access to center city Chicago. It also stabilized the regional traction business through consolidation. However, the

While collecting postcards of transportation subjects has been a popular pastime since the original postcard collecting era at the turn of the 20th century, one area that seems to have garnered a lot of interest recently is miniature railroading. As luck would have it, the postcard era began during the same time that miniature railroads took hold, and there are literally hundreds of cards to be found. Miniature railroading should not be considered the same as narrow gauge railroading. American 24" gauge (the width between the rails) in Maine and 36" gauge elsewhere were true commercial railroads in every sense of the word. They were not toys and moved traffic and passengers from point to point for purposes other than amusement.

As a rule, miniature railroads feature smaller-than-lifesize equipment and are operated on a closed loop circuit. Ranging in track width from 6" to 36" gauge, the only commodity they haul is people. Their primary role was to move people around amusement facilities, parks, zoos and fairs. Some were also owned by private individuals.

In the earliest days, they used very small live steam locomotives just like real railroads did. The primary builder in the 1890-1915 era was the Cagney Brothers Company out of New York City. The four

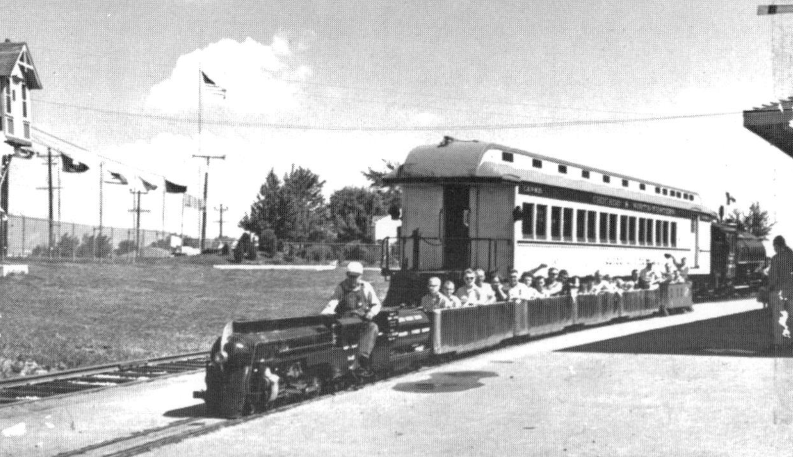

Above - One of Norm Sandley's live steamers at the little roundhouse of the live-steam Quinsippi Central miniature railroad in southern Illinois (and a full-size Burlington Route diesel loco in the background) Right - A small, homebuilt steam model of the 20th Century Limited plying the rails at the National Railroad Museum in Green Bay, Wis., in the 1960s.

Cagney Brothers marketed their engines in a variety of sizes, most using a 4-4-0 (four lead wheels, four main driving wheels, no trailing wheels) "American" class arrangement. With 1300 examples built, a Cagney engine is what is normally seen on pre-1910 postcards.

Thousands of well-skilled machinists in America during this era also meant some of the trains were home-built. These might have been constructed completely from scratch using homemade castings, or built from a kit. Regardless, all were a labor of love by a competent builder. One company that actually tried to make a business of live steam engine production after World War II was owned by a real train engineer named Norm Sandley, whose Riverside & Great Northern shops built 15" gauge trains in Wisconsin.

Live steam is not a toy, however, and the same maintenance any industrial boiler requires is needed for safe operation. Though most parks used live steam in their early days, those that did not desire the labor-intensive atmosphere turned to internal combustion. Many of these still *looked* like steam engines. The Detroit Zoo turned to engineering friends at the nearby Chrysler Corporation for their internal combustion trains in the late 1940s, which were modeled after the streamlined steam engines used on the Milwaukee Road's Hiawatha. Incidentally,

Above - Three engines meet on the Pinconning & Blind River line in northern Michigan in the 1950s. The owner of this railroad used it both for tourists and to haul fresh-cut logs out of his large property. Left - An MTC G12 using electricity for power is guided around a large layout set up in the Abram & Strauss department store in New York. This card is from sometime in the 1950s, and was used to advertise the equipment available for rental. Andrew Jugle collection

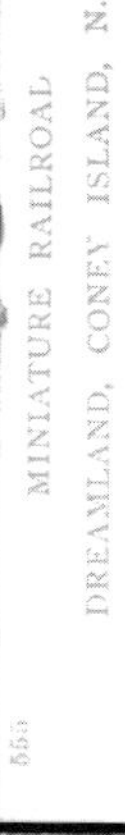

(above and top) Multiple live-steam Cagney locomotives were operating at Coney Island New York in 1905, and others are seen on the House of David park line in Eden Springs, Michigan circa 1920s. Some live-steam Cagneys have been restored, including one presently in use at the Strasburg Railroad in Pennsylvania. (left) On a scarce real photo post-card, a small strealiner gets ready to leave the depot in the 1940s. Based loosely on the Hiawatha, these locomotives were built for the Detroit Zoo by Chrysler and were powered by a marine-type internal combustion engine. Zoos and parks were the mainstay of miniature railroading.

these particular miniature trains continue to run in summer months to this day.

But the advent of the streamlined mass-production diesel for real railroading would spur on a major renaissance in miniature railroading after the second World War. The primary builder and marketer was a Glen Ellyn, Ill.-based company known as the Miniature Train & Railroad Company. Owner Paul Sturtevant had built his first train in 1928 and had marketed ride-on electric-powered trains as in-store rental rides during the 1930s. He created two popular models based around GM's Electromotive Division's full-size locomotives that took the amusement train ride to the next level. Classed as G-12 and G-16 (based on size), they could be produced in a variety of gauges and power ranges suited for each customer's need, and the company also marketed matching sets of streamlined passenger cars to go with them. In 1948, the name was changed to the Miniature Train Company (MTC for short), and the company produced its popular engines for many sites around the nation. They were profitable through the mid-1950s, but fell upon hard times due to market saturation and changes in the amusement business.

In 1958, MTC was sold to a man named Allen Hershell who in turn was bought out by a company named Chance Rides in the late 1970s. Hershell and Chance made most of the steam-type locomotives seen in park postcards from the late 1950s onward. While MTC's steamliners may have been popular, many parks still wanted a steam outline engine with internal combustion power. Chance's 4-2-0 type engines, modeled after the Central Pacific's **C.P. Huntington** locomotive of the 1860s, are by far the most common of the later steam types. Truth be told, once the initial cash outlay for a train and track was made, miniature railroading could quickly become profitable at .10-.25 cents per ride.

For collectors, the highest values seem to be coming from those cards that feature the postwar streamlined engines built by the Miniature Train Company. The MTC streamliner postcards actually have a wider base of interest than other miniature railroad

Mount Gretna's
Little Railroad

Before concluding this section, there is one other line which sort of bridges the gap between the miniature and full-size railroads. This was the short Mt. Gretna Scenic Railway in Pennsylvania, a four-mile 24" gauge line that connected the Conewago Hotel and Mt. Gretna Park with the mainline Cornwall & Lebanon Railroad station nearby. The line, which began in 1889, used 4-4-0 locomotives built by a standard locomotive manufacturer (Baldwin), and served the resort and a rifle range of the Pennsylvania National Guard in Lebanon County, near Harrisburg.

This little line proved to be a popular subject during the postcard fad, and quite a few different cards were made of the operation. Unfortunately, several passengers were injured when a number of young soldiers attempted to board the moving train at once. The subsequent derailment on July 11, 1915 ensued, and the line was permanently closed at the end of the season. The rails themselves were lifted forever in 1916.

Three examples of postwar miniature railroading. At top left, an MTC G16 engine on the five-mile line in Breckenridge Park in San Antonio, Texas, and, above, the Portland (Ore.) Zoo's Zooliner, modeled after EMD's experimental Aerotrain (this model is still running there today). Two internal-combustion styles are seen in the vertical card from Audubon Park in 1950s New Orleans. Note the Santa Fe-style "war bonnet" paint on the MTC G16 diesel, whose accurate graphics and hues were supplied by GM's Electromotive Division, which built the full-sized designs of the train.

postcards, and with good reason. Streamlined real train collectors, toy train collectors, locality-specific collectors, railroad line-specific collectors, collectors of amusement park and zoo memorabilia, and so on, are all in pursuit of these cards.

The chrome era translates these cards the best, as most linen miniature streamliner cards tend to suffer badly from poor re-touching. Real photo cards aren't often seen of this subject, though the House of David settlement in Michigan did enough that those are probably the most common of the miniature railroad cards. Some examples, of course, are much scarcer than others. Recently, thanks to eBay and other sites, many previously undiscovered cards have become available.   ✱

WORKIN' ON THE MODEL RAILROAD

Model trains were an occasional subject on picture postcards. The primary examples from the 1907-1915 postcard era were Christmas postcards showing children with toys, often including a train. Collectors hold these cards in high regard when depicting specific toys. There were also a few cards done to promote model train sales in later years. Any card mentioning or advertising classic tinplate-type, three-rail electric trains from the toy firms themselves would be in high demand from toy train collectors.

Some cards depicted layouts or collections; a couple of these are illustrated here. These are fairly scarce images; they are not easy to come by and, if they hold one's interest, would be well worth purchasing when available. The most common of the public display model train images were from the Roadside America tourist attraction in Hamburg, Pa. Most others would be considered desirable and scarce to interested collectors. However, like many postcards, this is a market with narrow demand, so prices remain reasonable on most cards.

Giving pause to admirers of classic electric trains would be this view showing dealer Frank Rochet's collection from the 1950s. The rarities include Lionel, American Flyer, Ives, Dorfan, and Buddy L equipment. To the right is an outdoor American Flyer set from the 1920s (top), a sprawling commercial model using Lionel equipment called Midget City, which was located in Sanford, Fla., in the 1940s (center), and a 1950s advertising card for a California-based Lionel-type layout called the Centinela Valley R.R. , mentioned in the books written by pioneering train collector Louis Hertz. Note the customized engines.

There is some disagreement as to when the modern postcard era began. Some like to begin it with the first photochrome cards (referred to as 'chromes' in the postcard hobby) that came into vogue just before the Second World War. Others would be inclined to say that it occurred when European-style continental cards became prevalent in the 1960s. For railroad collecting, my personal preference is to put the modern era as post-1965, which was approximately the time that the railroad hobbyist aftermarket began producing cards, and the railroads themselves had, for the most part, stopped doing so.

By the time the 1960s rolled around, the railroad industry was undergoing some significant changes. The money that had been generated during the war years was gone. Despite massive investment, passenger service had dwindled, much of it surviving more because of Interstate Commerce Commision (ICC) fiat than any desire on the part of the railroads themselves. In addition to the explosion of personal

(left) The Seaboard continued to issue cards for its New York - Florida trains until the late 1950s, perhaps in deference to its aging ridership, who still used postcards for correspondence. Meanwhile, the aftermarket began producing cards. At right, Ross Rowland's ex-Nickel Plate Berkshire engine gets under way out of Kansas City in 1969 as part of the High Iron Company's Golden Spike Centennial Limited. The train was painted and lettered for American Railroads as part of this celebration. Audio-Visual Designs, Don Wood photo. At lower right is a continental-sized card of the Milwaukee Circus Train; cards in this 4x6 size have only marginal collector interest.

auto ownership, jet planes were a quicker mode of travel and priced competitively. Meanwhile, the 'tyranny of the urgent' common to the modern corporate mentality rarely allowed one to take a business trip via rail unless it had an ulterior purpose.

The industrial heartland was also starting to downsize. Many finished goods, with the significant exception of automobiles, were now behind long-distance semi-tractors on the nation's highways. The railroad had countered with the unique concept of 'piggyback,' wherein a loaded trailer could be put on a high-speed freight and taken across the nation, but this was still often an uphill battle from a purely economic standpoint. Moreover, the ICC-ordained freight rate structures were still based on the time period fifty years prior, when the railroads had been the dominant form of transport. There was no easy way that trains could compete with the less-regulated trucking industry, and they suffered accordingly. Even today, there are railroad enthusiasts who still maintain a somewhat bitter feeling that the government was using the taxes received from the railroads to help build the competing airports and highways.

The postcard business was changing as well. Public tastes found postcards passé, and many of the postcard companies were losing business. The use of postcards for advertising had long since been surpassed by the color illustrations found in most periodicals by this time. The hobby of *collecting* antique postcards would not take off in earnest until the late 1960s. Collectors tended to be archivists rather than consumers.

Nonetheless, though the railroads rarely saw the need for postcards as a promotional tool by this time, there were some exceptions. The most important corporate cards were the painted Howard Fogg images

(above) The 1976 Bicentennial brought many unique paint schemes out of the woodwork, such as this high-nose Norfolk & Western SD45. To assemble a full collection of the special schemes from 1976 from the various producers is a challenge, though the prices are quite economical on literally all of them. Mary Janes, N&W corporate photo, card courtesy Norman Hechtkoff. (below) While many modern postcard images feature trains, some focussed on trolleys and interurbans. Few would deny that this Pacific Electric view from 1959 is a classic. Audio-Visual Designs, Leo Caloia photo.

equipment that had been donated to the city park or put on display at the downtown depot.

There were independent operators using even bigger locomotives and, with the blessings of a railroad's management, would operate these behemoths on the main line. Rail enthusiast Ross Rowland's restoration of Nickel Plate Berkshire 759 from the Steamtown collection in Bellows Falls, Vermont, in the late 1960s was considered the beginning of this. However, both the Southern Railway and the Union Pacific (which has always corporately rostered at least one steam locomotive since it began in the 1800s) both took up the charge and began running additional steam excursions themselves as a public relations boon. The UP continues to this day, though astronomical insurance rates and a diminishing number of suitable passenger cars have put most of the big steam engines once again back 'out to pasture,' so to speak. Like tourist trains, many postcards were produced of these excursions.

The third and final group would be the railroad aftermarket postcard producers, of which there were about a half-dozen. The first was Bob Fremming, who did commercial black-and-white litho and real photo cards during the latter half of the 1950s into the 1960s, with a variety of views and somewhat marginal reproduction quality.

The most prominent in the railroad hobby itself has been Audio-Visual Designs, which continues on to this day, having produced somewhere in excess of 1500 different views over the past 30+ years. These range from the corporate photography covered elsewhere in this book to current scenes that document contemporary railroading. What A-VD achieved was the near-complete documentation of the end of the passenger era and the beginnings of Amtrak in 1971, as well as

issued by the railroads, covered in the "Art & Artists" chapter. Among others, these special art cards were created by the Rock Island, Pittsburgh & Lake Erie, and M-K-T, or Katy, lines. In the 1950s and early 1960s, a handful of chrome color photo cards were also done for promotion by the Seaboard Coast Line, the Santa Fe, the Union Pacific, and a few other railroads.

The next group of major postcard producers would be the new tourist lines that had come into being as the steam locomotive disappeared from the American transportation scene. Fueled by the twin desire to preserve history and relive a bygone age, there were dozens of these short lines that would operate steam trains on weekends or as tourist attractions, often with a complimentary Old West shootout or Indian attack. These operations sometimes published several different cards each season, and some have become collectible in their own right, but their original goal was to promote the attraction. In addition, postcard producers were called on to create cards of static engines and the fading glory of first generation diesel power, plus other train, trolley, and excursion views. The company promoted its wares through the rail enthusiast press and the hobby industry, and used a variety of numbering schemes before settling on the letters RP followed by a series of digits. Owners Joe and Coleen Suo continue to offer cards for sale, and have even reissued some of the more popular cards.

Lyman Cox was also fairly prolific in the 1970s, with virtually all of the cards he produced related to the glory days of railroading prior to 1960. As mentioned in the corporate photo section, Cox published many railroad file images that had not been used before, both as postcards and as his Vanishing Vistas 6x9 series, using printers like Mike Roberts and others to ensure quality. When not using corporate photos, Cox had the small base of serious railfan photographers who had documented the end of the steam age and the streamliners in color. Today, Richard E. Cox offers some of these images as large format prints, and continues to market a portion of the popular Vanishing Vistas postcard series as well.

Mary Jane Rowe and her Mary Jane's Railroad Specialities is likely the best-known aftermarket railroad producer in the postcard hobby. The Mary Jane's postcards are still the most commonly seen issues in that venue, and cover an enormous variety of images. From a quality standpoint, the company's earliest cards were sometimes printed on uncoated stock and not always the best exposures, but do feature subject matter not available anywhere else. Mary Martin Ltd., a large postcard dealer in Perryville, Maryland, bought out most of the Mary Jane's Railroad Specialities back stock some years ago, and still has many (though certainly not all) cards available for purchase in brand-new condition.

Parlor Car Enterprises does high quality issues, focusing primarily on good railfan photography, and Meyer Postcard Company in

Roanoke has done several nice Norfolk & Western images from the final days of steam (one is seen on page 84 in the Corporate Photography chapter).

The latest entrant into the mix was Railcards.Com, based out of Alameda, California, but they appear to be out of business. These cards are often seen for sale on ebay in groups of 72. There were several other smaller firms that produced railroad cards in the last quarter-century.

As mentioned in the real photo section, there are certain photographers in the railfan hobby who have garnered notoriety. Among those in the recent color era would be Don Wood, Bob Collins, Jim Shaughnessy, Dave Sweetland, and a few others. The reprints of images by Ed Nowak and his corporate photos would also be on this list. Most of these cards can be identified by the shooter's name and his accompanying use of excellent light, good photo locations, and sharp focus. To date, however, this fame has not necessarily resulted in higher values on these cards.

The larger continental-size cards came into vogue in the mid-to-late 1960s. Today, most modern promotional postcards are done on this format, including Amtrak and tourist lines. While there is a small aftermarket for these, very few collectors seem to show interest in them, preferring instead to stay with the traditional 3.5 x 5.5 format. This is not to maintain that continental-size cards are forever worthless; they are simply not avidly sought after on the current collector market. This may change as the next generation of collectors arrives.

In conclusion, it is still possible to build a very substantial collection of the modern, standard-sized chromes. Some of the cards were issued in small numbers and distribution was often regional as opposed to national, meaning there is a solid challenge to obtaining some of them. Prices at online auction have been steep when a pair of collectors decide they are going to own the example regardless of cost, but otherwise they maintain a fairly flat, economical price range. ✳

The popularity of the postcard was assured by the time that the 1907 postal change occurred. The front of the card could now be used solely for the image. Both correspondence and the address could be written on the backside. As a direct result, collecting postcards became a very popular pastime nationwide until America entered the First World War. However, postcards were still limited by their very size and simple design. So the various postcard designers and producers began to look at creative ways of making their product lines more unique.

Perhaps the most interesting of these special cards from the pre-1915 era were the hold-to-light cards. These cards were printed in Germany and featured a special layered paper design. Slightly thicker than normal, they appeared to be very much like ordinary cards until held up to a bright light. The light then passed through die-cut holes in

Among the more unique cards would be the large-letter card from Lima, Ohio, where the company's famed Super Power locomotives were built. At right are two of a more serious nature: one a general admonition about auto safety, the other illustrating the aftermath of such an encounter. The latter was issued by the B&O and sent directly to drivers who ignored a crossing gate guardsman.

*O*ne of the most enduring railroad postcard scenes was of a bridge location at Sixteenth and Dock Streets in Richmond, Va., a site where the rail lines of the Chesapeake & Ohio, Seaboard Air Line, and Southern Railways crossed each other. On several different occasions during the century, professional photographers captured views of trains on all three levels. It is unique among railroad postcards in that the images span the various types of motive power used by the railroads, from the smallest steam engines of 1900 to the latest high-tech diesels of the late 1990s. Today, many of these views are still common, and six are pictured here. Incidentally, the earliest image (left) may have been done for the Baldwin Locomotive Works. Many of the scenes were produced by a local photograph outfit named Dementi. It is possible that real photo cards, which would be rare by any standard, could have been produced of these staged events as well.

the cardstock, creating illumination that showed through the moon, buildings, and other highlights. While hold-to-light (HTL) cards ran the gamut of subject matter, a handful did depict railroading, particularly in the New York region. As imagined, they are in demand by both railroad collectors and those people who focus on HTL issues. In fact, these cards are normally quite expensive due to the fact that prices are fairly well-established on many of them. HTL cards are not believed to have been produced following the first World War.

Another unique type of card was the fold-over type. These cards were usually two panels wide, although sometimes they would consist of three or more panels. Printed on a single piece of paper stock, each panel was the size of the normal postcard, so the card could then be folded down to normal postcard size, sealed with a small piece of tape and mailed. Obviously, these cards were somewhat fragile in nature; multiple opening and closing attempts could eventually cause the panels to separate. Trains were subjects on these cards, the most common being the group of four done by the Baltimore and Ohio

A fold-over card of the famed Horseshoe Curve in Pennsylvania. This photo, made sometime just after the Civil War, was still being used into the 1950s.

for their 1927 Fair of the Iron Horse (see page 42). Fold-over cards were never an extensively-produced medium, however, and are scarce by any standard. This is tempered by the fact that they are not in high demand by the general collector market.

The accordian-type postcard folder became popular very early on. This was a cardstock binder slightly larger than a normal postcard that held a series of views printed on paper stock. In virtually every case, the images inside would also be issued as normally-produced single postcards as well. The railroads saw this as a great opportunity since it allowed them to show a number of views along their travel route to help promote business, and were particularly popular among the railroads in the expanding Western regions. For the railroads, the era of the postcard folder ran from the first to the fifth decades of the century, fading away as passenger service declined. From a demand standpoint, those folders featuring views of trains passing through the scene will be more popular then those issued by the railroads which show simply scenic views. The ***Mononland*** issue on page 113 is a folder that has a higher level of interest today than most others.

Another unique card style was done for the Union Pacific/Southern Pacific where it crossed the Great Salt Lake in Utah. This card featured a small bag of salt attached to the edge of the card, usually with an image of a train crossing the causeway over the lake. Some other cards were produced with glitter, copper-ink windows, or other extra add-on pieces, though the process occasionally hurt the image.

Finally, a few cards were done to simply get a message across: use caution when crossing the right of way, come to an event or festiv-

ity, or notifying customers, 'your package has arrived.' In terms of unique illustrations, by far the most common are those showing oversized produce or livestock on train cars. There remains an endless variety of these, with the real photo manipulations done by several creative photographers being in the greatest demand.

All of these specialized items have varying levels of interest. As with most other railroad paper items, graphics will play a role in pricing. Mechanical cards, which had a moving tab or part attached to them, were created prior to the advent of the linen era, and are fragile. There are certainly some examples available featuring railroad subject matter. While few of the folders are in major demand, many collectors will have representations of these accordian-like cards in their accumulations, more for their novelty then any monetary value. ✱

CROSSROADS OF COMMERCE

THE CINCINNATIAN—B & O Deluxe Coach Streamliner

Two railroad-issued art postcards - An example of Grif Teller's PRR calendar artwork (left), and the B&O's new

General postcard hunters will often look for old cards that bear the imprinted signature by certain illustrators, which are known as artist-signed postcards. On a rare occasion, a train might be part of such a rendering. For railroad collectors, however, the most desirable artwork will be postcard images of trains themselves. The only exception to this rule would be the Winold Reiss images of Native American Indians done for the Great Northern Railway in the late 1920s, which are in demand by paper collectors from several diverse fields.

On the earliest postcards, the railroad illustrators are mostly anonymous. Some of the better art-type postcards of that time were shown in the previous section on limiteds. There were also several well-known artists in the field of railroad illustration. Often, the railroad would make use of artwork done for other types of advertising for their postcards. The Pennsylvania Railroad used several of Grif Teller's famous calendar renderings this way, as did the New York Central with its yearly images by Walter Greene. The Baltimore and Ohio used examples of company magazine cover paintings for identical sets done in 1927 and 1934. Later, the Union Pacific created a set of 12 cards showing western states with trains in action in the 1940s (see page 47). While the late Ted Rose was responsible for a set of postcards issued by the postal service only a few years ago, the most popular postcard artist for railroad collectors is Howard Fogg.

Fogg was born in 1917, and first began focusing on railroad art after a stint in the Air Force flying P-51 Mustangs during WWII. His first big account was with the American Locomotive Company (Alco) in the late 1940s, but his primary patron was a railroad management visionary named John Barriger. Barriger had been part of the reconstruction of the railroad industry during the Great Depression and into the Second World War. In the postwar era, he turned his attention to the Monon (CI&L), a dwindling enterprise that spanned from Louisville, Ky., to Chicago. As part of his modernization, he hired Fogg to paint a series of 18 images showing the Monon at work in its home state of Indiana. Barriger was known to use these postcards for personal correspondence as we shall see in the next chapter.

By the beginning of the 1960s, Barriger was in charge of the Pittsburgh & Lake Erie, a subsidiary of the sprawling New York

Railroad-issued art postcards by Howard Fogg are shown here. These examples of Fogg's mastery of the rail image range from the deiselization of the Monon (top), to the postcard book issued by the P&LE in 1964 (above), and a continental-sized postcard tribute from the famous UP calendar of 1969. The postcard at right from the P&LE is the author's favorite Fogg image of industry.

Central empire. Fogg, whose art was now illustrating advertising postcards for both the Rock Island line and the books of author Lucius Beebe, was again called by his friend. Barriger commissioned Fogg to paint almost every business the heavy-duty railroad served in the valleys of the Ohio River. This would include mines in West Virginia, the mill complexes of Pittsburgh and Youngstown, power plants, chemical companies, and so on. When completed, there were a total of 66 different Fogg images that the railroad published as a bound postcard collection in 1964, with two white-bordered images per page on serrated paper, as well as issuing most as single cards without borders.

Fogg would again join with Barriger for several cards on the Katy (M-K-T) Railway when Barriger came to straighten up that operation in 1966, including a number of cards done for the line's 100th Anniversary in 1970. During this time, Fogg also created what he personally considered the most epic work of his career: a series of paintings for the centennial of the Union Pacific in 1969. Most noted as a calendar, there was a set of larger-than-continental postcards on very thin stock of these 100th anniversary paintings that have proven hard to get.

He also did at least one postcard for the Union Tank Car Company, the Union Railroad (no relation), an advertising postcard for the H. Bairstow Company of Chicago, and others. Fogg died in 1996. Much of his life's work (thought to number approximately 1200 different images in all formats) is now sought after by many railroad collectors. *

As with most collectibles, the most desirable postcards tend to be those that have never been used, still in crisp, mint condition. Although printed on heavier stock than paper, the cards still often suffered from errant handling as they traveled through the mail serving their intended purpose. Nonetheless, there are instances where postcards are actually more valuable if they have been used. This is occasionally based on a rare postage stamp specimen, but more often it is due to a special cancel.

Prior to the advent of wide-scale commercial air transport, railroads carried an immense amount of the U.S. Mail. Special 'Railway Post Office', or RPO, cars were part of many of the trains between larger cities, and high volume areas such as New York-to-Chicago sometimes warranted high-speed trains of NOTHING but mail. These cars were equipped with special filing compartments that allowed postal personnel to sort mail as the trains traveled toward their eventual destinations. Sorted mail would be dropped off at stations along the route while additional mail would be picked up. In some rural areas, the post office itself might even have been located in the station. In the post-World War II era, the loss of this business was a hard blow to the passenger end of the railroad business as it was taken over by the trucking and airline industries.

Obviously, with millions upon millions of postcards in circulation during the first half of the century, some were can-

Here are a sampling of three RPO-type and special cancels. At top is a scarce real photo of Teresa, N.Y., with an Ogdenburg & Utica cancel. Below it a Santa Fe advertising card with an Albuquerque & Los Angeles RPO denoting train 18 (the eastbound Super Chief), which is also depicted on the card. At bottom is an unposted card with a special cancel from Corona, Colo., the highest point on Denver & Salt Lake line.

celled in the RPO cars. This is a specialized form of collecting; not all postcard or railroad collectors are going to have an interest in these items. However, they are scarce enough that they add a certain type of charisma to a card. Though they read 'RPO' in the cancel, the exact train issuing the cancellation can be hard to identify in some cases, since they are often just a train's number (i.e. TR 4). In some cases, a card depicting a certain train (such as the Super Chief or the Broadway Limited) and showing an RPO cancel could well be from that particular consist.

On special occasions, a group of cards might have been done with an RPO cancellation as a souvenir. Following the principle of the postal first day cover, railroads might stamp a postcard with a special RPO cancel. This occurred on a number of occasions with the inaugural runs of new trains during the streamline era, and was a common practice at the various railroad fairs and railroad exhibits during the 1930-1950 era. The special cancel would sometimes include an additional rubber stamp marking in the message area of the card that would state the exact nature of the occasion. These, of course, are highly prized by the collectors interested in them.

Finally, on very rare occasions, a card might show up where the message itself was important. An important person may have jotted a message down on a card, or an enthusiast might have had somebody important sign a card. The Monon card reproduced on these pages with a message from then-railroad President John Barriger is one such item.

Christmas Eve in Mononland

Chicago, Ill., July 8, 1952

MONON
THE HOOSIER LINE

I am greatly honored by having my name listed in such distinguished company in the 1952 roster of Railway Enthusiasts. Thank you for your vote of confidence. If your summer travels bring you to Chicago, please let Stanley and me have the privilege of extending you some Hoosier hospitalities.

John W. Barriger

GENUINE CURTEICH-CHICAGO "C.T. ART-COLORTONE" POST CARD (REG. U.S. PAT. OFF.)

CHICAGO
JUL-8'52
U.S. POSTAGE
POST CARD
PLACE STAMP HERE

Mrs. Jerome W. Atherton
Box 133
West Townsend, Massachusetts

While this is a specialized segment of the collecting market, it occasionally will attract a greater audience than railroad enthusiasts. In the earlier era of the postcard (pre-1930), there were many smaller railroads that had RPO cancels. An item from such a line would be of interest to a regional card collector, particularly if it is a local view of his or her specialty.

NEW YORK—16 HOURS—CHICAGO, VIA THE WATER LEVEL ROUTE

DAWN OF A CLASSIC

*F*ew *trains in North America had the prestige of the New York Central's* **20th Century Limited**. *Following its introduction in 1902, this New York to Chicago express run was considered the premier train nationwide for almost 60 years, and was literally unmatched in terms of its lavishness and opulence. As the streamlined era reached full swing, the NYC turned to noted stylist Henry Dreyfuss to design suitable shroudings for the latest Hudson-type steam locomotives chosen to power the train. The classic final product, introduced in 1938, literally became the defining work of transportation Art Deco design.*

On June 15, 1938, one of the ten special engines built by American Locomotive Company left Chicago at 5:00 PM, slated for arrival 961 miles away in Grand Central Terminal 16 hours later. Somewhere during that trip, the postcard seen here passed through the hands of the RPO clerks on board and was given a special one-day only rubber stamp commemorating that trip. While this card is one of the most difficult of the streamlined era to find (the well-heeled clientele of the Century were not often given to jotting correspondence on postcards), this particular RPO makes it a true rarity among railroad collectibles. ✳

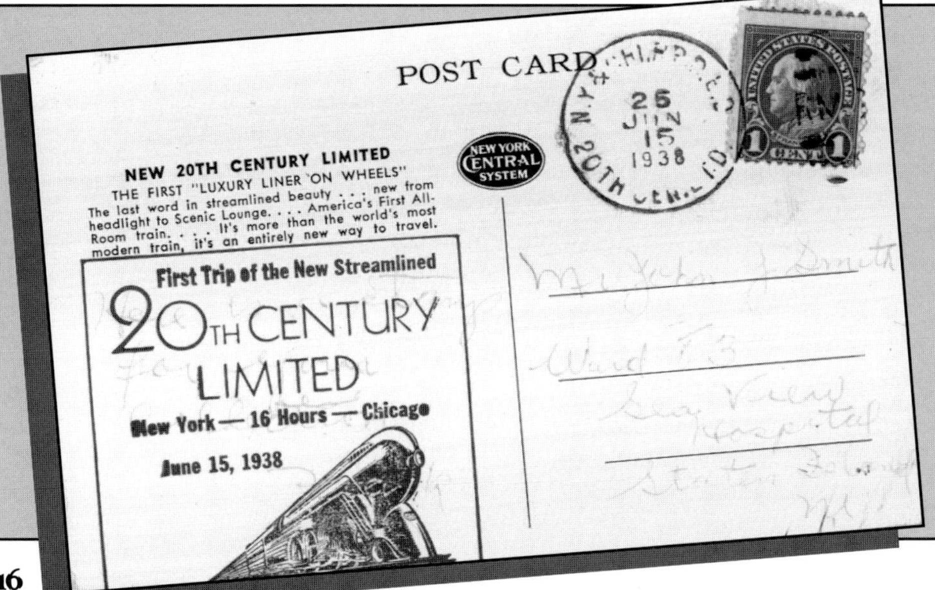

In all likelihood, if you have decided to read this chapter, you have something more than just a simple interest in railroading. Picture postcards represent a truly unique form of illustration, a practical object that was used everyday during the era of their popularity. They were produced in immense quantities, but were often discarded in the same measure, creating both rarity and demand in today's collectibles market.

The cards used to illustrate this book range from the common to the rarely seen; they were collected from a variety of sources over the course of a decade. Though I began formulating this book several years ago, cards came into my possession that were particularly well-suited for it even as the final drafts were being written. There were still others discovered at online auctions like eBay that I saw and bid on, but could not obtain. In the next few pages, we'll take a brief look at the hobby of antique postcard collecting and some of its facets. Listed in the column to the side of each page are some of the resources to help you begin your quest, increase your collection, or sell your family heirlooms.

Grading and Quality

The adage from the real estate market "location is everything" can certainly be modified to antiques as "condition is everything." While there are some techniques that can help restore paper goods like postcards, it cannot be stressed enough that owning the best examples available will make a collection more enjoyable. Postcards were sometimes tucked away to remain as pristine as they appeared when sold new, but more often than not, they were sent through the mail to be folded, spindled, and mutilated. Others were hung up with thumbtacks, used as scratch paper, stained, and heavily handled. As a rule of thumb, buy the best. When that isn't possible, the collector must make a personal decision about whether to purchase a particular card despite its flaws.

Some definitive guidelines for grading cards have been established. Susan Brown Nicholson's noted book on the hobby, *The Encyclopedia of Antique Postcards,* gives some excellent tips on how to rate postcard conditions. J. L. Mashburn's third edition of the *The Postcard Price Guide* lists basic grades as follows: M for *mint* (new stock), NM for *near mint* (light aging but almost like new), EX for *excellent* (mild handling, no damage, may be posted), VG for *very good* (many cards are in this condition - light creases or corner stubbing, posted or used, still presentable), G for *good* (heavy creases, soiling, heavy cancels, roughly used) and F for *fair* (anything worse than Good - tears, missing pieces, etc.). One final grade from my perspective would be P for *poor*, which is junk but may have a place in the railroad hobby due to rarity. As mentioned above, all of these sources recommend that the collector buy cards in the best possible condition.

Buying Postcards

There are many sources for buying railroad postcards. Of course, companies that still exist like Audio-Visual Designs out of Herkimer, New York, continue to supply high quality cards

POSTCARD PUBLICATIONS

Postcard Collector
700 E. State St.
Iola, WI 54990
www.postcardcollector.com
information & show listings

Barr's Postcard News
P.O.Box 601
Vinton, IA 52349
(800) 397-0145
information & show listings

POSTCARD SUPPLIES
See Mary Martin Ltd (p. 117)

Harris Gray
P O Box 246
Brookfield, MA 01506-0246
(508) 867-7210
www.postcardsupplies.com
storage supplies

ONLINE POSTCARD AUCTION SITES
www.ebay.com
www.playle.com

RAILROAD POSTCARDS
Regional Interest Histories
Arcadia Publishing
2 Cumberland Street
Charleston, SC 29401
843-853-2070
www.arcadiapublishing.com

to rail-oriented hobby stores and museums. If one enjoys looking at all kinds of postcards, many antique malls have a selection of cards someplace in their booths (though, I will note, railroad subjects are often few and far between). The rare Teresa, New York card on page 114 came from an antique store. However, if you are serious about collecting, there are really three major sources for cards today: antique postcard dealers, shows with postcards, and the Internet.

There are many antique paper dealers who specialize in postcards. If you are searching for certain subjects and regions, these people will be one of your best resources. Some dealers, like **Mary Martin Ltd.** in Perryville, Md., are full-time, full service storefront businesses. Others are part-time hobbyists who bring their stock out to postcard or paper shows. Still others open their homes by appointment, or sell only by mail order or approvals. Approvals are offered by dealers who will send out a batch of selected cards to a buyer. The buyer, who pays postage both ways, chooses the ones to keep, and returns the remainder with the payment. The **International Federation of Postcard Dealers (IFPD)** keeps a roster of their members online listing each one's methods of business at www.playle.com.

Postcard shows are another source, as are shows featuring railroad and transportation collectibles. The postcard show gives many dealers a chance to set up in front of a larger audience, and many great cards can be bought this way. Probably more than half of the cards in this book were purchased at shows. If you collect railroad postcards and have never had a chance to go to a postcard show, you will likely be amazed by what you find (and may be broke when you leave!). Railroadiana and book/paper dealers will occasionally have postcards for sale at those events, though this is more akin to hunting cards at antique malls - you may have to look at a lot of Lionel and HO scale model trains before finding someone with postcards for sale.

Then there is the Internet. Millions of people have awoken to the fact that buying and selling collectibles online is a great business. Postcards can be found at many sites in this medium; **Postcard Collector** magazine even has an advertising section devoted to promoting postcards 'on the net.' The largest auction site is eBay, www.ebay.com, which features 100,000 or more postcard subjects for sale every day. Sooner or later, just about every type of card imaginable comes up for sale on eBay; you just have to keep your eyes open. Ron Playle's postcard auction site also hosts several dealers and the complete IFPD member roster. I have been able to find some great purchases at www.playle.com.

I thought I would relay a couple of quick stories from my online adventures here, as I have bought and sold postcards and other items on eBay for several years. I recall one Ontario & Western card several years ago (which I wanted for this book) that I bid up to over $60.00 on eBay, and lost. Lo and behold, another one turned up at a postcard show only a couple of months later for…$3.00! On the other hand, the cards used to illustrate the C&O William Rittase section on pages 81-82 proved very hard to come by, even at shows. One afternoon, on a whim, I found a set of six on eBay and was able to buy the group for less then $20.00 including the postage. Like everyone else, I've paid too much for stuff on eBay, but I've brought home a share of bargains as well.

The moral is - keep your eyes open. If you find a postcard someplace that you feel you have to own (I like to refer to it as a haunting card) and you can afford it, by all means, buy it. However, if you are willing to gamble, you might get another shot at it. Some depot postcards have topped $300.00 on eBay when the action gets hot and heavy, but would have likely cost $25.00-50.00 or so in most retail situations. Auction fever is a large part of eBay's success; take care not to bid to unreasonable amounts. Good cards can also be part of larger lots offered for sale.

One nice aspect of eBay is the ability to ask the seller questions about condition and quality before purchasing. Also, check the seller's other auctions once you have made a bid. It is often possible to buy more than one postcard from a seller and get a combined shipping rate.

One final note before going forward concerns the mail order auction, where a dealer will list a selection of premium cards up for bid via mail or phone, ending the auction on a certain closing date. This is still one way to buy cards, though it is fading in popularity as the electronic auction grows. I bought the Pennsylvania S1 real photo card seen on page 32 via a mail auction.

Selling: Wholesale, retail and online

If you have cards to sell, you can do it several ways. As mentioned, there are the online auctions, where you put the cards up for sale yourself. It is imperative that, if you are selling an entire group at once, you individually list and illustrate as much of your lot as possible. Like all profitable enterprises, sites like eBay have been discovered by their share of unscrupulous people. Most knowledgeable buyers have gotten burned enough times that they will not bid large amounts on questionable or picked-over lots. If you choose to try and sell your cards one at a time, you will find the return is often good but can be very time-consuming. One solution that I have used is to bundle cards into groups by railroad, era, type, etc., and offer them as small lots focused toward a particular group of buyers.

Having access to a scanner or digital imaging equipment is very important if you plan to sell online. This is because most buyers will want to see the card before they buy it. Even if the subject is extremely rare or interesting, you may be cheating yourself out of a substantial amount of profit by not offering an illustration. An honest assessment of condition is also important. List any flaws, since most people will take your description at face value. Check your email often to see if any questions have been asked, and answer promptly. One final note is not to worry if the auction seems lifeless; many buyers will wait until seconds before an auction ends to place a bid in hopes of winning.

Should you decide the online auction is not for you, you can also take your cards to a postcard dealer, who will evaluate them and give you an offer based on a percentage of the estimated values on the cards. Depending on the assortment, condition, rarity and other factors, the dealer will be a good route to take if you are not interested in trying to sell a collection piece-

RAILROADIANA COLLECTING & HISTORICAL GROUPS

Railroad Collectors Assn., Inc.
550 Veronica Place
Escondido, CA 92027
www.railroadcollectors.org

National Railway Historical Society
P.O. Box 58547
Philadelphia, PA 19102-8547
(215) 557-6606
www.nrhs.com

Railway & Locomotive Historical Society
P.O. Box 292927
Sacramento CA 95829-2927
www.rrhistorical-2.com/rlhs/

ONLINE RAILROADIANA GROUPS
www.railfan.net

HISTORIC RAIL PERIODICALS
Classic Trains/TRAINS magazine
P.O. Box 1612
Waukesha, WI 53187-1612
www.trains.com

Railroad & Railfan
P.O. Box 700
Newton, NJ 07860
973-383-3355
www.railfan.com

meal, and would like to get a single lump sum for your cards. Don't expect the dealer to pay you a huge amount for common cards, however. If certain cards are in abundance and unlikely to resell in a reasonable time, the dealer's money is tied up in them. There may not be enough retail interest in the card to justify buying additional copies. A good example are most railroad cards from the 1933 World Fair. Most dealers are fair and will make very reasonable offers to buy quality materials. This is an easy way to sell postcards.

Storage/Handling of Vintage Paper

My current collection consists of 20 or so loose-leaf one-inch thick binder notebooks, with each volume focused on a particular subject, card style, or region. As your collection grows, you will find that multiple smaller albums are easier to sort through and review than larger ones. For actual storage, I use an archival 8.5" x 11" type of page made by Fleer that holds four cards. I place each card into a semi-stiff acetate-type plastic sleeve so that I don't need to touch it again. This is particularly important if you like to hold individual cards, since it prevents damage to edges and corners when sliding them in and out of the storage pages. The binders themselves are stored in a cool, dry bookshelf with good ventilation. It is not good to subject any paper collection to serious changes in humidity or temperature.

Careful handling is a must when sorting and archiving cards. Despite the fact they are on heavy paper stock, they are easily damaged. Though it is not necessary to wear cotton gloves, as some people do when handling photo film, if you are prone to perspiration or use lotions, be forewarned you can easily stain the cards with your fingers.

Focusing Your Collection

Most people have a wide variety of interests, and since postcards come in so many different categories, it is easy to have a variety of subjects in one's collection. Personally, I have everything from gas and bus stations, to reptiles, to race cars among my postcard files. However, it is probably wise (mentally and financially) to not try and collect everything in every category that interests you.

Obviously, there are certain cards that I've been willing to pay

more for, cards for what I call 'focus' categories. In railroading, these might be of a particular region that interests me, or a type of artwork or card style that has been hard to come by. Of course, most collectors tend to like a little bit of this and a little bit of that. This is fine, but maintaining a focus on even a small sub-category can help make a collection more enjoyable. One of mine has been the railfan-issued RPPC, or real photo postcards, with handwritten notations, since I consider them to be little miniature artworks printed by the masters themselves.

You can focus your collection by deciding what you are trying to accomplish with it. This could be the record of a certain time, the history of a locale, or the abundance of cards related to one railroad or another. One gentleman I knew paid some fairly large sums for cards that I would not have considered worth a tenth of his price, but the collection he amassed was amazing in scope because it dealt with one railroad line in one region - he had the depots, the industries, the scenery, and more, even collecting extra examples of some of the retouched, reissued cards done during the course of several decades. His focus made that collection worth a lot more as a whole, and it certainly was the only one so complete on that railroad. The cards he paid the most for took on a special significance because he obviously knew the subject and therefore its rarity.

Conclusion

Collecting postcards is a terrific hobby. It is one that can be done to suit any budget. Good items are still to be discovered, and many of the people involved in postcards are knowledgeable and pleasant. I greatly enjoy the time I spend creating and viewing my collection, and know that, even now, there are still many cards out there that I have never seen. It will never become a boring pursuit… ✳

Postcard collecting as a hobby had its origins in the early years of the last century, but took its place among serious hobbies in the 1960s. Since that time, terminology has been developed that is widely understood among enthusiasts, and these definitions help the collector and reader understand exactly what is being presented, especially critical when buying or selling postcards. Here is a brief chart explaining some of these terms; additional explanations can be found in the postcard-related volumes mentioned in the Bibliography section at the end of this book.

Artist Signed (AS): While not a direct subject matter with railroading, artist-signed postcards are printed UDB or DB cards that show the signature of the artist on the artwork. Most of these postcards depict people, and date from the 1900-1920 era. In railroading, the premier artist shown on postcards is Howard Fogg, whose work was done in the post-WWII era.

Chrome: Kodachrome film had a profound impact on photography, and by the 1940s, postcards were being produced using offset color photography. The early 1950s found the railroads and others using this format, and the advent of specialty railroad postcard publishers allowed tens of thousands of others to be produced. Some chromes are very common, while others are in demand. These should never be referred to as 'real photo' postcards, as they are not printed from the original transparency or negative onto photographic paper.

Deltiology: The hobby of collecting postcards.

Detroit Publishing Company / Detroit Photographic Company (DPC): A specific branch of collecting based around the Detroit Publishing's "Phostint" cards, which used a proprietary Swiss stone lithography process to print very realistic color postcards from the UDB era of 1900-1907 though the early 1920s.

Divided Back (DB): America's greatest postcard collecting fad began in earnest after Congress allowed the backs of postcards to be divided by a line in 1907, with the right half for the address and the left for the message. The vast majority of older cards are from this time period of the postcard 'craze,' which lasted from 1907 to approximately 1915 and the outbreak of the Great War. As an aside, the war also ended the import of many high-quality cards that had formerly been produced in Germany.

Hand-Tinted: These are black-and-white litho cards that were detailed or toned with watercolor-like inks (obviously, the inks had to be weather-proof to circulate in the mail). These are often higher-quality cards then normal lithos, and some are amazingly beautiful creations by the unknown artists.

Linen: Linen postcards are what come to mind for many when thinking of "Greetings From" large-letter postcards. A high rag-content paper allowed the used of bright colors, and is named for this texture. It is in this era that most of the best streamliners and steam-to-diesel transition postcards were produced. After beginning in the 1930s, linen cards were produced into the late 1940 and early 1950s. This process was superseded by the chrome-type postcard.

Lithographic Postcards (Litho): this term normally refers to postcards done without the use of colored ink or retouching, and are basically offset-press black-and-white images. They can be found in either UDB or DB formats, and were the cheapest to produce.

Multiview cards (MV): Postcards featuring more than one image.

Pioneer cards: Very early postcards done prior to 1898, when Congress authorized the private printing of postcards.

Postmarked - PM: A dated postal service cancellation.

Postwar: Following the end of World War II, after 1945.

RPPC cards are singular images produced by amateur photographers. These cards will show no signs of the printing process (offset press patterns). Once disdained in the hobby, for railroad and postcard collectors in general, these are often the highest-demand cards today.

Undivided Back (UDB): Postcards produced between 1901, when the term Post Card was first allowed by the postal service, and March 1, 1907. The backs of these cards were reserved solely for the address, meaning any message had to be written on the front, or illustrated, side of the card.

White Border (WB): In the mid-1910s, with Germany no longer supplying cards, American firms took over, and many used a border around the edge so that the cards could be produced to less-exacting standards. Quality suffered as a result, especially with heavy retouching on the older images. This era traditionally ranged from about 1915 through the 1930s when the linen process took over, but various cards with borders around the outside edge have been produced throughout the entire postcard era. *

Private Mailing Cards (PMC): Postcards done from 1898 to 1901 and labeled as Private Mailing Cards.

Railway Post Office - RPO: A dated postal cancellation done while enroute on a mail or express train.

Real Photo Post Card (RP or RPPC): These are black-and-white postcards printed directly from a negative to special photo papers labeled as Post Card. These should not be confused with either lithographed cards nor color cards of any era. The development of photography in the earliest days of the 20th century coincided with the postcard craze; many

Above - A wonderful real photo multiview of Chicago (now called Willard), Ohio. Of interest is the fact that each view shown on the card was also an individual postcard release from this supplier. This card was created by taking a group photo of the postcards in the studio, using lighting from above and left to provide the shadows.

While ascertaining exact values on collectibles is always arbitrary, this basic price guide will give the reader an idea of what some of the cards used in this book might appraise for. This dollar-range figure is my personal opinion, based on recent show and internet sale estimates and prices. Condition for these values would range from Very Good to Excellent (minimal wear). Therefore, better cards may bring more, poorer cards may bring less.

Page	Image/ Age	Value $
Cvr	Jersey Central Blue Comet 1930, daylight express	10-20
1	CB&Q Pioneer Zephyr w/first day cancel 1934	18-35
3/127	Kennebec Central Togus ME 24" narrow gauge (detail) 1910	10-20
4	Interurban car and depot - Crawfordsville, IN 1909	6-12
6	St Louis MO train leaving depot 1906 b/w litho	3-6
6	PRR Pennsylvania NY-Chicago Special 1902	4-7
6	Cumpson-Prentiss Coffee w/ Empire State Express 1906	7-12
7	Ill. Iowa Car Service mailing card 1904	1-2
8	NYC New York Central - streets of Syracuse NY 1905	8-15
8	DL&W Lackawanna Hoboken NJ Tunnel 1906 b/w litho	5-9
9	DL&W Lackawanna Oxford Furnance NJ depot RPPC	10-20+
9	NYO&W Ontario & Western Bloomingburg NY b/w litho	7-12
9	Union Terminal - South Station Boston 1903 embossed litho	2-5
10	Trolley crash lithos - Charlton, MA 1905 (set of two)	7-20
11	P&R Reading train Boyertown PA 1906 RPPC	8-15+
12	Incline - Lookout Mountain Chattanooga TN 1905 DPC	3-6
12	On The Frisco (SL-SF) Adamsville AL 1909 DPC	7-12
13	Mt Washington NH Cog Railway engine 1910 DPC	3-7
13	Ephraim Shay Train Engine MI 1910 DPC	5-10
14	PRR Pennsylvania Huntingdon PA depot 1914 wb	7-12
14	NYC Grand Rapids MI Depot 1908 color	8-12
15	NKP Nickel Plate Tippecanoe IN 1908 RPPC	8-15
15	LE&W Lake Erie & Western Tipton IN 1910 litho	10-20
16	Kansas City MO Union Depot DPC 1910	3-7
17	PRR Pennsylvania Concordville PA 1908 hand-colored litho	10-20
18	NYC New York Central Carmel NY 1910 b/w litho	8-20
18	Cincinnati OH Union Terminal - Exterior 1935 RPPC	5-10
18	Cincinnati OH Union Terminal - Interior 1935 linen	3-6
18	ATSF Santa Fe Del Mar CA 1940 RPPC	10-25+
18	LV Lehigh Valley Sayre NY 1940 b/w litho	8-15
19	NH New Haven Bridgeport CT 1915 wb color	4-8
19	Wichita KS - CRI&P / SF/SL lines 1909 color MV	4-8
19	Wichita KA - AT&SF / MP lines 1909 color MV	5-9
20	Grand Central Station NYC 1912 litho	2-4
20	PRR Pennsylvania Station NY 1920 b/w litho	2-5
20	PRR Pennsylvania Station Interior NY 1930 linen	3-6
21	PRR Pennsylvania Station Train Inside NY DPC 1910	7-15
21	NYC Electric vs Steam 1908 b/w litho	6-10
22	MP Missouri Pacific Sunshine Special 1915 color litho	12-20
23	RDG Reading Wall Street Special 1925 wb	7-12
23	LV Lehigh Valley Black Diamond 1910 wb	7-12
24	B&O Baltimore & Ohio Capitol Limited 1920 RR issue	7-12
24	C&A Alton Limited one panel Mail Baggage 1904	8-15
24	C&A Alton Limited complete train (not shown), five panels	75-125+
24	LV Lehigh Valley Kitchen multiview 1906 color litho	10-20
25	CMStP Milwaukee Road Olympian bi-polar 1918 RR issued	15-30
25	CB&Q Smoking/Lounge Car Interior 1910 RR issued	7-12
26	UP Union Pacific Overland Limited 1909 Fred Jukes picture	5-9
26	N&W Norfolk & Western Pocahontas 1938 linen	8-15
26	WAB Wabash Banner Blue 1938 linen	8-15
27	CNW Chicago Northwestern 400 Train 1935 linen	7-12
27	CNW Chicago Northwest 400 Interior (steam era) linen	8-15
28	NYC New York Central Castleton Cutoff 1926 litho RR issue	5-10
28	PRR Pennsylvania Broadway Limited color litho	5-8
29	CMStP Pioneer Limited 1908 MVRR issued	10-18
29	NP/CBQ Northern Pacific/Atl. Express 1909 MV	10-18
29	CBQ Burlington Lines West via Western Pac. 1912 MV	10-18
30	CBQ Burlington Zephyr Prairie Du Chein WI 1934 RPPC	10-25+
30	NYC Commodore Vanderbilt/Dewitt Clinton 1937 RPPC	8-15
30	GN Great Northern Empire Builder Puget Snd 1947 linen	5-10
31	CBQ Twin Zephyrs Advertising Card 1936 litho	8-15
31	UP Union Pacific City of Denver Reno NV 1937 RPPC	10-25
32	NYC Mercury Streamlined steam 1937-40 RPPC	8-15
32	PRR S-1 Experimental Crestline OH 1945 RPPC	10-25
32	RDG Reading Crusader advertising card 1939 RR issue litho	8-15

Page	Image/ Age	Value
33	CMStP Hiawatha Steam Tomah WI 1936 RPPC	12-25
33	CMStP Milwaukee Rd Hiawatha Alco DL109 1940 linen	10-20
34	GM&N Gulf Mobile Northern Rebels by ACF 1939 litho	8-15
34	GM&O Gulf Mobile & Ohio Alco DL109 1941 linen	10-20
35	CNW Chicago North Western 400 EMD E6 1939 linen	5-10
35	CNW Chicago North Western 400 Interior 1938 linen	7-12
36	KCS Kansas City Southern Belle 1940 linen w/logo	10-18
36	KCS Kansas City Southern Belle Interior 1940 from folder	6-12
36	KCS Kansas City Southern Belle complete folder(not shown)	25-50
37	IC Illinois Central City of Miami 1945 linen	10-20
37	IC Illinois Central City of Miami Interior 1945 linen	15-25
38	WAB Wabash City of Kansas City EMD 1951 linen	10-18
38	WAB Wabash City Train Interior 1951 linen	8-15
39	UP Challenger Diner Interior 1940 linen	10-25
39	UP Overland Streamliner in mountains 1939 linen	8-15
40	ATSF Santa Fe Super Chief EMD E7 1945 linen	5-10
40	ATSF Santa Fe Scout Interior 1945 linen	8-12
40	ATSF Santa Fe Steam over Cajon Pass 1935 linen	3-8
41	ATSF Santa Fe Line of Streamliners 1938 litho	6-12
41	ATSF Santa Fe Giant Compound Engine 1906 DPC	3-7
42	B&O Baltimore & Ohio Railroad Fair 1927 litho	2-5
42	B&O Baltimore & Ohio Rail Fair fold over litho 1927	6-10
42	B&O Baltimore & Ohio Railroad fair 15-cards set w/ env.	50-75
42	NYC New York World Fair DeWitt Clinton 1940 linen	3-7
42	CNW/UP San Francisco Worlds Fair Entrance color litho	2-6
43	CBQ Burlington Zephyr Display 1934 litho	2-4
43	B&O Color Magazine Cover postcard 1934 litho	5-10
43	B&O Color magazine Cover 14-card set 1934 w/env.(not sh.)	75-100
43	GN Great Northern Steam Engine 1909 b/w litho	8-15
43	UP Big Boy Chicago Railroad Fair 1949 b/w litho	2-4
43	NP Northern Pacific EMD and Minnetonka 1949 b/w litho	2-4
43	PRR Pennsylvania 7002 Worlds Fastest 1949 color litho	1-4
44	DMIR Duluth Ore Trains Hibbling MN 1906 color litho	4-8
44	--- Strip Mining Hazleton PA 1920 wb	4-8
44	--- Valley Coal Mine Leechburg PA 1908 color litho	7-12
44	PRR Pennsylvania Ashtabula Docks OH 1908 color litho	8-15
45	PRR Pennsylvania Ashtabula Docks OH 1920 wb	5-10
45	B&LE Bessemer Push-Pull Ore Train 1909 color litho	7-12
45	--- Steel Mill at Night, Youngstown OH 1940 linen	4-8
45	---- Steel Mill Genesee NY 1906 color litho	8-15
45	NYC New York Central Willys-O Toledo OH 1915 wb	7-12
46	WM Western Maryland Challenger 1951York Fair color litho	7-12
46	SL-SF Frisco Steam 4500 Series 1944 linen	6-10
46	ATSF Santa Fe FT Servicemen 1942 color litho	3-7
47	SBD Seaboard Freight Advertising Card 1945 color litho	8-15
47	UP Union Pacific State Painting 1940 color litho	5-12
47	UP Union Pacific State Painting set of 12 1940 color litho	60-85
48	UP Union Pacific Big Boy PR Cheyenne WY 1950 chrome	2-5
48	GN Great Northern Steam Hillyard WN (WA) 1909 RPPC	10-18
49	ERIE Erie Caboose 1970 A-VD chrome	1-4
49	N&W Norfolk & Western Newport News VA 1905 DPC	3-8
49	NCStL Dixie Line loading Hobbs Island AL 1910 b/w litho	12-20
50	NG Narrow Gauge logging Tuolumne CA 1909 bw litho	8-15
50	WV&N Wenatchee Valley Log Train 1910 RPPC	10-20
51	---- X Gas / X Ray Oil Advertising card 1908 RPPC	8-15
51	NYC New York Central train/truck 6x9 Van.Vistas	3-10
52	MEC/B&SR trains at Hiram ME 1930s pic,1960s print litho	4-8
52	MEC depot Farmington ME w/dual gauge 1912 bw litho	12-20+
52	Rangeley Lakes advertising region w/train 1930s linen	8-15
53	B&H railcar #3 at Bridgeton ME 1930s bw litho	12-20
53	Edaville Railroad work train, postwar color litho, 1940s	3-7
53	WW&F Head Tide ME bridge train accident 1905 color litho	8-15
54	C&S Argentine Central at Mt. McCellen 1908 color litho	4-8
54	C&S Georgetown Loop Detroit Publishing Co 1907	6-12
54	RGS Ophir Loop Trackage - Telluride, CO 1912 wb	5-10
55	DRGW Dual gauge-Royal Gorge- Detroit Pub 1905	4-8
56	Santa Cruz Railroad, dual gauge depot with tr. 1910 color lith	7-15
56	SP Southern Pacific steam engine, narrow gauge 1952 RPPC	3-7
57	EBT East Broad Top 1900s train/1960s reprint RPPC	3-7
57	W&W Washington PA depot with train 1912 color litho	7-12
58	ET&WNC real photo Doe River Gorge 1908- RPPC (each)	8-20
59	WP&Y streamliner on dock 1960s chrome era	2-4
59	RGS Galloping Goose, CRM museum, 1970s A-VD	2-4
60	NYC Hudson on turntable, Elkhart IN 1940s RPPC	10-20
60	CBQ coal tower, Ferguson IA 1910s RPPC	6-12
61	FEC Pres. H. Flagler @ Key West Jan 22nd 1912 color litho	15-25
61	FEC train on Key West bridge FL, 1920 wb	3-7

Page	Image/ Age	Value $
61	D&H/ERIE Starrucca Viaduct PA w/engine 1908 color litho	8-15
61	NYO&W steel bridge, Cadosia NY 1910 b/w litho	7-12
62	McAdoo tunnel contruction with workers, 1908 color litho	10-18
62	SOU Southern train at Natural Tunnel, VA 1925 RPPC	7-12
63	Westinghouse shop floor, engine construction 1910 bw litho	8-15
63	VGN Mightest Engine in World Virginian Rwy bw litho	8-15
63	MILW generator facility, Piedmont, MT 1915 litho	7-12
63	GN First train, first Cascade Tunnel, WA 1915 RPPC	10-18
63	N&W Norfolk & Western train, Bluefield WV 1912 wb	8-15
64	MEC Mountaineer diesel, Crawford Notch 1930s bw litho	10-18
64	PRR Horseshoe Curve postcard folder, 1940s/1950s bw litho	7-15
65	Railroad yards, Kansas City, KS, 1910 colr litho	3-6
65	CRI&P Interior, Rock Island shops,1907 (blank bk)blue litho	6-12
66	S&W South & Western construction photo 1909 RPPC	15-25+
66	CRR Clinchfield train on Copper Creek 1913 RPPC	8-15
66	CRR Clinchfield construction photos 1908-10 RPPC each	7-15
67	CRR train on Copper Creek - detail from p.66	NA
67	NYC New York Cen.shop crew, unidentified 1910s RPPC	4-8
68	RGS Rio Grande Southern Galloping Goose, each RPPC	15-25
69	UP Union Pacific new Challneger engine, 1930s RPPC	6-12
69	RGS Galloping Goose, Richardson CRM ph,1940s RPPC	12-20
70	SP Daylight steam streamliner, set with env/1938 RPPC	12-30
70	SP Daylight steam streamliner, single from set RPPC	5-12
71	CP Canadian Pacific double-head train 1920s RPPC	4-8
71	WP Eastman photo, Feather River Cnyn, 1920s RPPC	7-12
71	CRI&P 4-8-4 action photo, Dick Kindig, 1940s RPPC	6-12
72	PRR yard crew with switch engine, unid., 1910 RPPC	5-10
72	LOG logging crew with Climax, Everett WA, 1908 RPPC	15-25+
73	UP wreck City of San Francisco clean-up 1939 RPPC	10-20
73	SPS/GN railroad yard flooded with engines, 1930s RPPC	8-15
74	GN Great Northern snowplow Windom MN 1909 RPPC	8-15
75	NYC K5a Pacific roster, Dean photo, 1930s RPPC	8-15
76	B&O steam train action MD, W. Price photo, 1947 RPPC	7-12
77	DRGW mail train, Otto Perry photo, 1939 RPPC	8-15
78	CNW four-train commuters, Pontin photo 1930s RPPC	7-12
79	MP Missouri Pacific Consol, Foster photo, 1930s RPPC	7-12
80	SP Southern Pacific City of Denver PR photo, 1937 RPPC	15-25
80	UP Interior Photo, Challenger Diner, 1938 RPPC	8-15
81	FORD Rouge River Mill overview w/trains 1920s RPPC	6-12
82	C&O Wm Rittase - turntable w/engines 1940s RPPC	15-25
83	C&O Wm Rittase - engine line-up, sunrise 1940s RPPC	8-15
83	C&O Wm Rittase - hump yard w/hopper, 1940s RPPC	8-15
83	C&O Wm Rittase - coal mine with car load, 1940s RPPC	8-15
84	N&W locomotive portrait photo, 1950s/1970s print chrome	3-6
84	CNW streamliners in Chicago, 1940s,AV-D 1970s chrome	3-6
84	SP Sunset Ltd, Alco in southwest, 1940s/Cox 1970s chrome	3-6
84	SP new Shasta Ltd Deco interior 1940s RR issue chrome	3-6
84	IC Illinois Central City and steam, 1950s RR issue chrome	3-7
85	NYC streamliner West Point, Link photo, 1960s RR issue chr.	5-12
85	NYC Pacemaker w/Mohawk eng., 1940s, VV 6x9 chrome	4-10
86	MILW righting a boxcar, Lil. Bell, 1909 bw litho	5-10
86	SP cab forward locomotive crash, pre 1915, RPPC	7-15
86	CV Central Vermont train splitting switch, 1930s RPPC	6-12
87	DRGW boiler explosion, Kindig photo, 1950, each RPPC	6-12
87	CRR head-on Clinchfield wreck, unidenified, 1910s RPPC	6-12
87	VGN head on steam atop electric 1913, poor expos RPPC	8-15
88	SP snowbound train on Donner Pass, 1952 each RPPC	6-15
88	GN first train after avalanche, identified 1910 RPPC	12-25+
88	Tank car explosion, head-on wreck, unid, 1910s RPPC	6-12
89	ATSF New Mexico washout, cars 1930s, unidentified RPPC	5-10
89	ATSF rail car off bridge, Randolph, KS 1915? RPPC each	15-25
89	NYC 20th Century Ltd wreck,St Johnsville NY 1920s RPPC	12-25
89	PRR telescoping cars, Mt Union PA 1917 fatalities RPPC	15-25
90	Interuban - Warsaw IN street, litho Photoette 1910 bw litho	12-25
90	Lake Shore line passing under w/train, OH 1912 color litho	8-15
90	Oregon Electric depot w/train, Harrisonburg, OR 1912 RPPC	20-35
91	Pontiac MI street scene w/street cars, 1907-1912, bw litho	7-12
91	Interurban car barn, unidentified, 1900s-1910s RPPC	5-12
92	series Delaware Water Gap, Detroit Pub. 1908, ea. DPC	4-8
92-93	series Delaware Water Gap, Detroit Pub. 1908, group of 8	25-65
93	McKeen 'windsplitter' car, NY line, 1910s, color litho	7-15
94	Cincinatti trolley incline, Det. Pub. 1900s DPC	6-12
94	Jefferson plane w/trains, Mauch Chunk PA 1900s color litho	7-15
95	Mt Lowe trackage, Mt Lowe CA 1900s Detroit Pub color	4-7
95	Key System cars, Berkeley, CA 1910s, color litho	10-20
95	Aroostook Valley, Washburn, ME depot, 1908 RPPC	20-35+
96	Illinois Terminal, postwar streamliner, 1940s orig. chrome	3-7

The shortest of the Maine 24" lines was the five-mile long Kennebec Central, and this restaurant also served as the depot at one end of the line. This scarce view is in high demand on the railroad postcard collector market. Also seen on page 3.

No volume of this nature could be done without the reference materials that have made the information available. Below is a basic selection of the books that were used to help make *Rail Mail* possible.

Specific books related to postcards and postcard collecting
Mashburn, J.L. - ***The Postcard Price Guide***. Colonial House Publishing 1997. ISBN 0-885940-03-3 - *postcard identification*
Nicholson, Susan Brown - ***The Encyclopedia of Antique Postcards***. Wallace-Homestead 1994. ISBN 0-87069-730-7 - *postcard collecting*

Specific books related to railroading on postcards
Grant, Roger - ***Ohio's Railway Age in Postcards.*** University of Akron Press, 1996. ISBN 1-884836-19-4.
Grant, Roger - ***Railroads in the Heartland.*** University of Iowa Press, 1997. ISBN 0-87745-600-3
Grant, Roger - ***Railroad Postcards in the Age of Steam.*** University of Iowa Press, 1994. ISBN 0-87745-465-5
Railroads in Early Postcards. Volume 1 Upstate New York (Palmer, Richard & Harvey Roehl); ***Volume 2 New England*** (Boothroyd, Stephen and Peter Barney). Vestal Press, New York - out of print.
Boothroyd, Stephen ***Down by the Depot: Southern New England*** Cranberry Junction, 2002. ISBN 0-9714961-4-5

Chapter 1 - Ol' 97
Jensen, Oliver - ***Railroads in America.*** American Heritage Publishing Company 1975. ISBN 0-07-032526-X McGraw Hill - *general information*
Hughes, Jim - ***Birth of a Century***, Tauris Parke Books, London, 1994. ISBN 1-85043-646-0 - *Detroit Publishing, W.H. Jackson history.*
Beebe, Lucius & Charles Clegg - ***The Age of Steam***, Rinehart & Company, 1957. LofC 57-5215 - *early steam railroading history*

Chapter 2 - Down by the Depot
Alexander,Edwin - ***Down by the Depot***, Clarkson N Potter, 1970. ISBN: 1112679669, *general depot information until 1920.*
Stilgoe,John - ***Metropolitan Corridor,*** Yale University Press, 1983. ISBN -0-300-03042-8 - *depot use philosophy and rail building development*

Chapter 3 - The Limiteds
See Jensen and Beebe/Clegg, above
Withuhn, William - ***The Spirit of Steam***. Smithark Publishers, 1995. ISBN 0-8317-5511-3. - *vintage steam train history and illustration*

Chapter 4 - the Streamlined Age
Schafer, Mike and Joe Welsh- ***Classic American Streamliners***, Motorbooks International 1997. ISBN 0-7603-0377 - *streamlined train history data.*

Chapter 5 - Fast Freight
Kaminski, Eric - ***American Car & Foundry Company 1899-1999,*** Signature Press 1999. ISBN 0-9633791-0-0 - *freight car history*

Chapter 6 - Narrow Gauge Fever
Hilton, George - ***American Narrow Gauge Railroads***. Stanford University Press, 1990. ISBN 0-8047-1731-1 - *the definitive resource of narrow gauge history.*

Chapter 7 - The Backshop
See Grant, Stilgoe, Hilton above
Goforth, James - ***Building the Clinchfield***. Overmountain Press 1989. ISBN 1-57072-028-2 - *specific information on CC&O construction*

Chapter 10 - Wreck and Disasters
Reed, Robert - ***Train Wrecks***. Superior Publishing 1968, LoC: 68-13249

Chapter 11 - Taking the Trolley
See Grant, Jensen, Stilgoe above

Chapter 12 - Miniature and Model Railroads
See Grant above. **Special thanks to L. Andrew Jugle for MTC information, *published in the Train Collectors Association Quarterly - 2001-2003***

Chapter 15 - Art and Artists
Hill, Ronald & Al Chione, ***The Railroad Artistry of Howard Fogg***. Cedco Publishing Company, 1999. ISBN 0-7683-2112-3

Geoff Stunkard, 40, is a career photojournalist whose previous media efforts include editing, designing and publishing magazines, primarily in the automotive field. His work has been utilized in dozens of magazines throughout North America. An accomplished photographer, he has also contributed pictorially to several of the nation's largest railroading periodicals. *Rail Mail* is his first book. His company, Quarter Milestones Publishing, is based in Johnson City, Tennessee, where he resides with his wife, his three children, and a lot of postcards.